The Bottom Lines 2018

52 More Memorable Lessons in Leadership

Tom Zender

Copyright © 2018 Tom Zender
All rights reserved.
ISBN-13: 978-1985887954

Endorsements for Tom Zender's Work

"Tom articulates well the principles necessary to create a business culture and value system that provides the supportive environment for individuals to successfully collaborate, innovate, and deliver great results."
— Fred Anderson, former CFO of Apple Computer

"Tom's understanding of both business success and spiritual values has led him to the knowledge that the two are not separate entities - they are two sides of the same coin, and he deftly shows their integration."
— Deepak Chopra, bestselling author of *The Seven Spiritual Laws of Success*

"Tom Zender is an astute business author and educator. His enlightened work is drawn deeply from his own experiences as a successful business leader. He brings that expertise into the academic world as well. Tom teaches with authenticity and wit."
— Dr. Wendy Campbell, PhD University of Southern California, Professor of Instructional Design for Arizona State University and Capella University

"Tom Zender masterfully raises the consciousness and confidence of people and their organizations."
— Jack Canfield, co-creator of the *Chicken Soup for the Soul* book series; bestselling author of *The Success Principles*

"Zender explains how to leap ahead of the field by taking the most important leap of all: recognizing the power of your inner spirit to create breakthroughs you might not have ever thought possible."
— Marianne Williamson, New York Times bestselling author of *Return to Love*

"You were a distinct asset to General Electric. Your ability to communicate is outstanding."

– Kenneth G. Fisher, former Vice President of General Electric

"You know going in that he's an accomplished business leader and mentor with an impressive record of success and achievements. He's sincere and authentic. He is humble, kind and appreciates being in your company. He's a good listener. If he has an ego, he hides it well. He's a role model leader."

– Don Henninger, former CEO and Publisher, *Phoenix Business Journal*

Dedication

The Bottom Lines 2018: 52 More Memorable Lessons in Leadership is dedicated to the generous CEO's and business mentors who have enriched my career by sharing their wisdom, providing their unselfish guidance, and by giving their steadfast devotion to my success. I deeply thank you, always.

Also, this book is dedicated to the readers of my weekly column, *Leadership Lessons,* in the digital edition of the *Phoenix Business Journal*. I am indebted to Chief Editor, Ilana Lowery, Digital Editor, Tim Gallen, Managing Editor, Patrick O'Grady, and Publisher, Ray Schey. They gave to me the privilege of writing weekly about the key element of all businesses – real leadership.

And, not to forget my cat, Angel, my faithful Muse who inspired me in writing all of my books, including this one.

As always, I am indebted to my wife, Wendy Zender, Ph.D., and so many business friends who have supported me in creating this *The Bottom Lines* series of books.

Table of Contents

Endorsements for Tom Zender's Work

Dedication

Table of Contents

Leadership Lessons 1 - 52

Preface

Acknowledgements

About the Author

Leadership Lessons 1 to 52

#	Lesson
01	Party time: How smart leaders celebrate employee success
02	What's your real problem: Are you solving the right one?
03	What do our desks tell us about leadership styles?
04	Business momentum: How leaders build the energy of success
05	"The Next": A continuum of leadership mastery
06	Leadership and the five "Laws of Bigness"
07	Branding feelings: Why marketing leaders do it
08	Enter the new mind of leadership
09	Gutless leadership: When courage caves

10	Leadership and close encounters of the third kind
11	How successful leaders teach motivation
12	Why hope is dead in business
13	Uncovering major myths about leaders
14	Are you elevating expectations?
15	Managing fear before it manages you
16	Essentialism and the business of less
17	The art and science of a business model pivot
18	Gratitude is a daily business
19	See how insight helps leaders learn
20	How to strangle your inner critic
21	Don't forget to open the gift of receptivity
22	Out with stagnation, in with reinvention
23	Write your future resume now
24	Watch out, here comes "neuroleadership"
25	Dump dumb goals and get SMART
26	Here are assumptions that will kill your business
27	This is how to defy uncertainty
28	The tyranny of vagueness
29	Women, leaders, and sledgehammers on the ceiling
30	Don't sit on it – standup for fast progress
31	Ending the terminal uniqueness of "no competition"
32	Your disruptive consciousness drives a new business era
33	Goodbye networking, hello connecting, and 5 ways to do it
34	Your business is failing (and you don't know it)
35	Getting results by harsh demands, effective expectations, and powerful intentions
36	Be respected - 9 unbearable reasons why you are not
37	Unambiguous disagreement and its creative power
38	Stupefying courage as the guts of startup success
39	Loose dots, fuzzy connectors, and clear visions
40	Repairing the ruins of strong skills and bad behaviors
41	Here are 5 ways to be an Early Adapter (not Early Adopter)

42	Ditch mediocrity and join "The Accountables"
43	Stop stalling and get your action in gear
44	Swing from loss to profit in 5 easy steps of follow-through
45	Purge old stuff and make room for more profit
46	See how failure is another word for success
47	Big cracks in your company vision and how to repair them
48	When business drama ends, leadership maturity begins
49	Short circuit negative energy - free yourself of complaints
50	Assassinate confusion with five bullet questions
51	Employee disengagement vs. best companies to work for
52	Too busy playing manager to be an effective leader?

Index

How to Order More Books

Preface

I am a Professional CEO Mentor. I continuously meet great leaders in my work, learning valuable lessons along the way. During my business career, I have collected hundreds of business lessons from my mentors, leaders, clients, and others. These teachings are brief, simple, powerful. And immediately useful.

The Bottom Lines 2018 is devoted to sharing more of the best lessons I have learned from a wide audience of business people: leaders, managers, and you.

Rather than the typical laborious business writings that we encounter, I write in a more conversational way – because I find that business wisdom is easier and more interesting to read and remember. Brevity counts. So does a touch of humor.

My business path began with General Electric and Honeywell, and moved through midsize and startup companies, and a global nonprofit organization. My leadership roles included CEO, senior VP, and board member in Fortune 500, NASDAQ, Toronto Stock Exchange, and other companies.

Today I am a professional CEO Mentor & Business Coach. Additionally, I mentor Arizona State University faculty members and students who have startup businesses, as well as serving the Maricopa County Community College District, the Center for Entrepreneurship and Innovation, the advisory board of Ottawa University's business school. And, I write a weekly column, *Leadership Lessons*, for the Phoenix Business Journal.

I have had a taste of everything on the broad buffet of business. Mostly satisfying. But with some occasional heartburn, too!

The Bottom Lines 2018 includes a wide variety of lessons from different business functions. Above all, they are useful for building better business. Proven stuff.

Each lesson ends with a short summary, *The Bottom Lines*. Here is the one for *Leadership and the five "Laws of Bigness."*

The Bottom Lines

Play big. Follow the Five Laws of Bigness: Vision, Culture, Action, Failure, Results. Your business will be irresistibly attractive, work intensely, build huge momentum, create opportunities from mistakes, and achieve great results. Bigness is better.

Acknowledgements

Thank you, all of my memorable business mentors at General Electric, Honeywell, Ottawa University, and many others.

I am grateful to those mentors who taught me to mentor others as my way of giving away what I learned.

And, yes, I thank my "anti-mentors" who unconsciously convinced me about many attitudes and behaviors that I do not want to emulate. Ever.

I thank hundreds of business writers who have produced the mass of books, articles, columns, and other publications that have so positively influenced me.

Thank you so very much to many business and personal friends for giving me ongoing support to bring *The Bottom Lines Series* of books to business readers who seek new ways to improve their leadership skills.

Thank you to the team at CreateSpace, Kindle Direct Publishing, and Amazon for their focused and expert assistance to help me to transform this book, and the other books in this series, from a vision into a reality.

Above all, I am forever grateful to my wife, chief supporter, and editor, Dr. Wendy Zender, Ph.D., University of Southern California. Wendy is gifted in helping me transform good ideas into something readable and useful. She should be. She is a graduate university professor who reads a continuous stream of doctoral level theses from her students. I think I am one of them!

About the Author

Tom Zender is a Professional CEO Mentor and Business Coach in Phoenix, Arizona.

He held leadership roles at General Electric and Honeywell, and has been a senior vice president in publicly held corporations, New York Stock Exchange and NASDAQ listed. Tom was the CEO of a startup technology company and he was president and CEO of a global nonprofit that serves over two million people globally.

His corporate board experience includes NASDAQ, Toronto Stock Exchange, and OTC listed public companies. Tom held nonprofit board positions with Ottawa University and the Forum for Corporate Directors.

In his CEO and senior vice president roles he held profit and loss responsibility for every business function.

Tom writes a weekly column, *Leadership Lessons*, for the Phoenix Business Journal, mentors faculty and students who have startup businesses at Arizona State University, and is an advisor to Paradise Valley Community College. And, he serves the Maricopa County Community College District's Center for Entrepreneurial Innovation (CEI), and is an advisor to the business school of Ottawa University.

He has spoken to business audiences of over 1,000 people in more than 20 countries.

Tom Zender is a graduate of Ottawa University with a B.A. in Business in focus areas of Leadership, Marketing, and Information Technology.

His first two published books were Amazon bestseller e-books about business ethics:

- *God Goes to Work* was among the top ten e-books in business ethics listed by Amazon.com. Published in 2010 by John Wiley & Sons, it was widely distributed in the United States, Canada, the UK, Australia, and India.

- *One-Minute Meditations at Work.* Published in 2011 by Hay House/Balboa Press, it was among the top 5% of all e-books sold by Amazon.com.

His third and fourth books, *The Bottom Lines 2016: 52 Unforgettable Lessons in Leadership* and *The Bottom Lines 2017: 52 More Motivating Lessons in Leadership,* are prequels to this book – part of the growing *The Bottom Lines Series* of books.

Tom's email address is tomzender@me.com and his website is www.tomzender.com.

Leadership Lesson 1

Party time: How smart leaders celebrate employee success

Not just rewards. Recognition. Being identified publicly as a contributor to success ranks high in the list of employee "satisfiers." Higher than fair pay. Annually, employees in Massachusetts rank being appreciated as a number one contributor to their satisfaction. Of least importance? Pay and benefits. Read on.

Surveys of 2.5 million employees in 90 countries conducted by Sirota Consulting over a 10-year period revealed that just 50% felt appreciated after their successful work.

And, psychology researcher Shawn Achor found through surveys in over 50 countries that when teams are given just one daily dose of recognition and praise, their productivity goes up by 30 percent. Huge.

Beyond simple praise

It is obvious. The time and cost to offer verbal and written recognition and gratitude to individuals, teams, and organizations for work well done is minimal. It is so easy we might overlook it. Don't.

There are other levels of appreciation available to leaders, managers, and supervisors that can be offered. Here are some:

Informal recognition – just walk up to the individuals and groups that deserve appreciation and verbally thank them; the sooner the better so that they connect recognition to their performance.

Planned appreciation – have a party. Hold recognition meeting, serve some snacks and cake, and visibly recognize those who deserve it; video stream it to other locations. Hold the same events in remote locations and video stream it around.

Special events – hold employee-of-the-year and team-of-the-month recognitions. Publish this good news and photos in company e-newsletters. Hang lobby and hallway plaques of recognition.

Recognition gifts – learn what employees like. Maybe a bonus, gift certificates, dinner for the employee and their spouse or other guest. Perhaps it is a special parking place or some time off. In some situations it might be a free trip for two. Be creative.

Reward risk taking – Tata Corporation of India looks beyond "failures" and sees challenging innovation and fearless trials supporting an entrepreneurial company spirit. They celebrate with their "Dare to Try" awards for out-of-the-box thinking. And learning new valuable information.

"Celebrate what you want to see more of." – Tom Peters, business author

Does it really work?

Over 800 HR leaders drawn from the Society for Human Resource Management (see note at end) (SHRM) were surveyed about their programs for employee recognition. Here are some of their inputs:
- 90 percent noted it positively impacted engagement.
- 86 percent said it increased employee happiness.
- 84 percent indicated it improved employee relationships.
- 68 percent stated it helped employee retention.

Beyond the simple thanks for good work, expressing company culture via creative recognition programs for employees is fundamental to motivating and retaining good employees. Hint: recognize and reward often.

Some companies share the good news about their star employees with customers, vendors, and surrounding communities.

Case in point

The CEO of ProSites, a web design firm, rewards hard work with paid retreats to exotic locations, visits to fine wineries, and fun limo rides around Hollywood. These motivators have helped reduce employee turnover. Oh by the way, sales have doubled.

The bottom lines

Party time! Implement good employee recognition programs. Lift up your good individual and team performers. Hold period and special events and do special things for them. Appreciation is at least as important as pay. Raise productivity and lower turnover. Grow your business and have fun doing it. Often.

Leadership Lesson 2

What's your real problem: Are you solving the right one?

Radar like. We find business problems and then apply resources to solve them. Or, the problems find us and we go to work on them. We work through problems or decide to work around them. Sometimes we abandon them. Worse, we avoid them. Costly.

What is a problem? An unexpected blockage to progress toward an objective. Unable to launch a new product. A stalled production line. Running low on cash. Great employee leaves. Tough new competitor. Endless.

Stop. Before we react to a perceived problem, respond to a deeper diagnosis of it.

What if?

Suppose the perceived problem is not the real one. And perhaps the quick solution is not the right one. An examination of all the possibilities by an adept team can better isolate the core issues. And devise optimum solutions.

Classic case. A fabric manufacturer experienced random infrequent soot-like stains in some of its cloth. The suspected facility, materials, machines, and staff were not the real problem. Then, the area outside the building was investigated. An adjacent railroad side track was found with a smoking diesel locomotive infrequently passing directly under an air intake into the factory. Problem defined. Solution, a new air intake. Case closed.

"Half the solution to any problem lies in defining it." – Dr. Phil McGraw, psychologist

Method to the madness

Kepner-Tregoe, Inc. contributed a classic process to problem solving. Their problem analysis method involves five steps:

1. Define the problem as it is perceived
2. Lay out the problem in detail
3. Establish possible causes
4. Test the most probable cause
5. Verify the true root cause

The perceived problem of failing to launch a new product on time might not be the product. Could it be the market? Or marketing? Or packaging? Or distribution? What if it is price, terms and conditions, service, availability of parts and materials for production, quality. Worse, what if the problem is several of these conditions all at once? Time to find out. Find the real problem(s). Fast.

A good question

Powerful questions can help sniff out the greater truth: is there a broader problem we should be looking at; is this problem really a problem and does it need to be solved; does this problem need to be solved right away; does this problem effect other areas; is this solution the best one?

"We thought that we had the answers; it was the questions we had wrong." – Bono, lead singer of U2

Right problem, wrong solution

Moneyball the movie, illustrated a potentially wrong solution to a big problem. In 2002 the general manager of a problematically weak Oakland Athletics baseball team was urged by ownership to use a traditional scouting solution in finding better players. But the Athletics' salary pool was too small to attract known top talent. Right problem, wrong solution.

Instead, the GM found a new statistical solution (sabermetrics) to hire unknown, undervalued, but promising players for the team.

The method was a home run. The Athletics then won an American League record 20 consecutive games. Right problem, right solution.

The bottom lines

What's your problem? The real one. Don't solve the wrong problem. Dig deep, find the right problem and everything about it use powerful questions. Team solve it. Don't walk away from problems. Go head on. Creatively.

Leadership Lesson 3

What do our desks tell us about leadership styles?

Cluttered desk? Clean desk? If our desks could talk, they'd have stories to tell. And we should listen. The organization and content of our desk tell us reams about our leadership styles. Creative leadership and operational leadership. Leaders of projects and leaders of people. Look at your desk.

What do Mark Zuckerberg, Founder/CEO of Facebook, Tony Hsieh, CEO of Zappos, and Max Levchin, co-founder of PayPal, have in common? And what is one common characteristic of Albert Einstein, renown physicist, Steve Jobs, founder of Apple Computer, and Mark Twain, author?

Cluttered desks.

Theory of creation

University of Minnesota research suggests that the "messies" are free to engage in innovative thinking and work. Free of organized constraints. Yet, they seemed to know where to find whatever they needed. Some form of "organized chaos."

They created radically new ideas, products, and services by organizing solutions out of a seeming swirl of information. They were not bothered by having a need to categorize, file, and organize information. They focused on solving problems. Big ones.

"If a cluttered desk signs a cluttered mind, of what, then, does an empty desk sign?"
– Albert Einstein, physicist

Neat freaks

Then there are those who have more sparsely populated desks. They are organized and know where everything is located. These people are timely, dependable, and normally can be depended upon to get important things done on time.

These employees function well in operations, production, finance, accounting, and maintenance, where time governs many decisions and actions. Facebook has an exceptional Chief Operating Officer, Sheryl Sandberg. Her desk looks organized.

"I am a very visual person, so my environment is important to me. If my environment is messy, I can't think clearly. I don't like clutter."
– Alexa Von Tobel, American business woman, author

Dynamic desks

We can make a choice. When we need creativity, be messier. And when we need organized action, clean up our desks.

Here are some tips to better organize our desks when we need to:

Separate important clutter – keep the clutter you need nearby, but not on your desk. Seriously consider trashing the clutter you do not need. Make room for newer stuff.

Build an aging pile – stack paper files that you are not quite ready to part with in a chronological pile. Every quarter throw out the oldest 25%. You won't miss it.

Get a big waste basket – use it to make deposits into it regularly. Keep it next to your desk. Ask the maintenance team to empty it every night. Don't look back.

Have one incoming pile – put all new items into one stack and use things from the stack as you need them. Periodically throw out the unused items.

Scan stuff – build digital files. They can be found more easily, duplicated, stored in multiple places, communicated to others. And have more room for good desk clutter.

And, we can do the same things with our digital files. Move them off our digital desktop into folders and backup discs. Use the digital trash can.

The bottom lines

Listen up. The messy desk will tell you, "You are creative, don't clean me." The organized desk will remark, "You are ready for action, don't clutter me." You can do both. Choose what works for you. Creative, operational, or both. Clutter or clean.

Leadership Lesson 4

Business momentum: How leaders build the energy of success

In motion. The business is moving and gaining speed. After significant effort the new company, division, or product is growing. It has momentum. But our tendency can be to then sit back and watch. As though it has a life of its own. It doesn't. Smart leaders build the momentum. How?

Energy. Add more resources to the existing momentum. To keep something good going and growing. Multiplying success.

"When you find yourself in the thickness of pursuing a goal or dream, stop only to rest. Momentum builds success." – Suzy Kassem, philosopher, writer, film maker

How Sam did it

Sam Walton founded Wal-Mart by targeting customers as his center of attention. This focus was the powerful launching pad of momentum that rocketed the company into the stratosphere of high-growth, high-profit corporations. United States and global.

Walton walked with customers, talked with customers, and discovered their needs. These early small-town customers lived in the southern U.S. Like Sam. So, he planted the first stores in smaller communities where large competitors did not exist. Blast off.

Lower labor costs, cheaper facilities, no competition, and an array of fair-priced goods created momentum. Constant improvement in all areas of the business built more momentum. The world's largest company by revenues. Over 11,000 stores.

Riding the rocket

$P = M \times V$. Momentum equals mass times velocity. Good leaders know that adding energy to something that is already big and fast, will get even bigger and faster. Here are some types of energy to add:

Knowledge – learn everything there is to know about your industry, existing customers, potential customers, your team, and core business functions. Top to bottom.

Communication – get to know everyone inside and outside your organization. Make friends, gather information, spread information, build long-term relationships

Test – try out new ideas for products and processes on others. Before you launch them. Get feedback. Make something that is good, better. Kill bad ideas and save money.

Enthusiasm – it is free energy to inject into the organization. Infectious, it helps overcome obstacles, propels teams to greatness, and rubs off on customers.

Rewards – honest praise for work well done is another free fuel for building momentum. Beyond praise, gifts and monetary rewards carry a big message. "You are appreciated."

Advantages – the winning uniqueness's of your business. As many as possible. Technology, product, service, price. Keep adding advantages for more momentum.

Flexibility – nimble, turn-on-a-dime, pivot. Your radar is always on and when changes are needed, you can address them quickly. Respond to shifts faster than anyone else.

Value – the sum of all factors that bring customers and keep customers. Quality, availability, service, features, price, more. Above all, your team. People.

Goals – ever bigger. Our Olympians don't just train to win – they train to break records. Set audacious, but achievable objectives. It is an irresistible attraction for great teams.

Dead rocket

Do nothing. Momentum will eventually die. A rocket running out of fuel will climb a bit more but will soon fall. A business with slowing momentum will eventually stop. Dead.

The bottom lines

Get momentum. Be a leader and launch a new business, division, or product. Add momentum quickly. Pour more energy into every aspect of the business. Rocket to the upper altitudes of accelerated growth and sustainable success. Keep building more momentum. Be unstoppable.

Leadership Lesson 5

"The Next": A continuum of leadership mastery

Meeting ended. Progress reported and noted about a project, an objective, or the overall business. Areas of concern discussed. Notes taken and prepared for distribution after the meeting. But a critical question was not asked. What?

"What are the next steps?" Good leaders will ask this question and request the answers. During the meeting and especially at the end of the meeting. Every time.

"Successful people maintain a positive focus on their past successes – and on the next action steps they need to take to get them closer to the fulfillment of their goals." – Jack Canfield, *New York Times* bestselling author

Inaction and inertia

If the ball is rolling, kick it again. Feeling good at the end of a productive meeting is great. But failure to ask about subsequent actions reduces all-essential momentum. We are easily led into inaction following good progress. A slowdown can end a good project. Or business.

Even if there is no next step, at least the question has been examined. And some new opportunity might arise that can add value to the business, team, or product.

A good leader keeps things going and growing by asking, "What's next?" Always.

The five "W's"

At the end of virtually any kind of meeting the leader and others should ask, "What are the next steps?" Allow everyone to respond. For every identified action these Five W questions should be asked (and recorded in the meeting notes):

1. What is the action – explain what needs to be done in enough detail for meeting attendees to read and understand when the meeting notes are sent out.

2. Why is it important – is each action step really needed, can it be less in scope or does it need to be more in scope, what objective does it support, and what is its priority.

3. Who is responsible – define what one person is to manage the action step, what resources that person will need, and the level of authority they have been granted.

4. When is it due – lay out the completion dates for each milestone within the action. It is important to gain agreement from the action team leader about the dates.

5. Where is the next meeting – what location and what time. Keeping the same day, time, and place creates a certain "rhythm of progress" for many projects.

Add these Five W's to meeting notes and publish to everyone who needs to know. Before the next meeting publish an agenda. Some meetings might be by phone or video conference – no difference. Follow-up matters.

Apple, Google, and "The Next"

Apple assigns a DRI (directly responsible individual) who is accountable for a given task. Every action has a DRI. This eliminates confusion about who is tagged to move the action forward. Clarity counts.

Google has a defined decision maker in each meeting. Business velocity matters. Consequently, decisions do not wait for meetings. If a decision is needed, hold a meeting.

In both companies, the next steps are clear and happen quickly. Look at their results.

The bottom lines

Get "The Next." Strong leaders conclude meetings with, "What are the next steps?" Anoint a leader for each action and publish the list. Include answers to the Five W's. Hold follow-up meetings. Add more next steps. Keep going, keep growing. What's next?

Leadership Lesson 6

Leadership and the five "Laws of Bigness"

Size matters. Tall and agile basketball centers dominate. Massive railroad engines pull enormous loads. Large buildings house thousands of tenants. Big companies dominate markets. And the economy. The Fortune 500 largest companies represent nearly 75% of the United States Gross Domestic Product. That's big.

The Laws of Bigness define five critical areas of business: Vision, Culture, Action, Failure, and Results. And they influence visibility and viability, organization, momentum, knowledge, and results. Whoever suggested that small is better missed the point.

"Bigness is Better" – Thomas Leonard, American businessman

Law of Bigness #1 – Vision

Big vision creates an irresistible attraction. A magnet. For top employees, investors, collaborators, vendors, and other needed resources.

Steve Jobs held a vision for a future that went far beyond computers. It incorporated a highly integrated, seamless system of computing, media creation, education, music, communications, watches, applications, stores, and more.

Add beautiful packaging, inviting marketing, and stellar service. All baked into Apple.

Law of Bigness #2 – Culture

Big culture means a conducive operating environment where people are willing to go all out to build a bigger better business. A place to express creativity and service.

Larry Page and Sergey Brin established a culture that continues to rank it as a great place to work. A resort-like campus, free food bars, and meditation rooms (and optional courses about how to meditate).

Add challenging contemporary technologies to bring to market fast. Go big. Go Google.

Law of Bigness #3 – Action

Big action ignites organized motion to build momentum. Focused activity to increase the velocity of business. Fast profitable growth is the target. The right steps at the right time.

Sam Walton talked to potential customers, looked at competitors, sized the market, and went to work. His calls to action engaged employees to create a new kind of retail store. In small communities – and then everywhere.

Add low prices, little competition, and a magical logistics system. Welcome to Wal-Mart.

Law of Bigness #4 - Failure

Big failure leads to major learning, knowledge, wisdom, and opportunity. Better ideas emerge, new products are birthed, and big markets are penetrated.

Henry Ford endured his three failed auto companies. But he learned what did not work and absorbed what was worth keeping. Then, assembly lines were developed, production processes made efficient, and prices minimized.

Add over-paid employees and minimum prices to consumers. Go further in a Ford.

Law of Bigness #5 - Results

Big results produce more big results. Momentum builds and more new products and services are launched. Everything speeds up and the business reaches an altitude above competition.

Herb Kelleher had an idea for a radically new kind of airline. He tossed tradition, put his employees ahead of customers, adopted one type of aircraft, had employees rotate through different roles, and drove to jet-speed growth and profits.

Add low prices, fun flights, great customer experience. Fly with Heart on Southwest.

Law of Smallness

Small businesses are significant, too. They provide 75% of new jobs in America – 50 percent of our workforce. And, many small businesses are acquired by large businesses. To help bigness.

The bottom lines

Play big. Follow the Five Laws of Bigness: Vision, Culture, Action, Failure, Results. Your business will be irresistibly attractive, work intensely, build huge momentum, create opportunities from mistakes, and achieve great results. Bigness is better.

Leadership Lesson 7

Branding feelings: Why marketing leaders do it

A name. So you think that a brand is about remembering a name. A company, product, or service. True, but there is more. When you hear a name, how do you feel? Strong brands evoke strong feelings. Including the "I gotta have it" urge that propels buyers to the checkout counter. What about other feelings?

Trust. Trust is the foundation feeling. We bond with businesses, products, people, and places we trust.

"Great companies that build an enduring brand have an emotional relationship with customers that has no barrier. And that emotional relationship is the most important characteristic, which is trust." – Howard Schultz, Starbucks CEO

Feeling dominoes

One good feeling leads to another. When we trust a brand, other feelings are added. Positive feelings about quality, special features, usability, service, and overall value.

Loyalty. That is the sticky feeling that keeps us coming back for more. The stronger our composite feelings about a brand, the more we are inclined to continue buying from that company and their products. Even when a competitor has strong offerings.

It is as if we form friendships with our favorite places of business. We feel good when we visit them. Frequently.

Anticipation uplift

There is an upbeat sensation when we foresee satisfaction. Even if we do not want some product or service being offered to us. But we are emotional, feeling shoppers and buyers. We anticipate feelings of satisfaction. "I will feel better after I purchase this."

Astute marketing leaders understand this. They build promotional messages that drive our emotions – including hoped for satisfactions. Additional satisfying feelings that we anticipate from our purchases include safety, affluence, beauty, trendy, part of something important. Happiness? Check!

A higher vibration. Our purchases can foster feelings of magic, intrigue, adventure. And power.

Play the loyalty card

Recently, *Forbes Magazine* identified the top brands with the most loyal customers. No surprise, these names are appealing to millions of customers. And many are global companies. They represent those companies and their products that strongly appeal to the feelings of their customers.

AT&T, Ford, Hyundai, Avis, Domino's, Dunkin' Donuts, Google, Konica Minolta, National Football League, Discover, Air Canada, Facebook, Kellogg's, Exxon Mobile, Nationwide, Travelocity. And many other famous names.

Some of the new entrants to the list include Under Armor, Reddit, Lyft, Footlocker, Nature's Valley, Kashi, and Anthropologie. The new brands in the list demonstrates that buyers seek alternative brands that better satisfy their emotional expectations. Anticipated satisfactions.

Products, people, places

Apple brands everything and everyone in their corporation, integrated. The company first appeals to our emotion of trust. Loyalty to Apple is extraordinary in a highly competitive industry. Their growth and profitability boosts them to one of the largest corporations in the world.

iMac, iPad, iPhone, iPod, iWatch. Every product is branded. Ease of use, sleek design, high function, seamless integration, reliable, value-priced, exceptional service.

Even Apple's people are branded. Knowledgeable, inviting, no-push service, thorough. And the retail stores are branded. Quiet, uncluttered appearance. Comfortable places for training and service. Ditto by phone, online, and email. Good feelings.

The bottom lines

Brands. Feelings. Bind them together. Begin with trust and extend into buyer feelings of anticipated satisfaction, value, utility, service, and more. Brand the business, products, people, and places that customers will want. Powerful branding creates customer loyalty. For good.

Leadership Lesson 8

Enter the new mind of leadership

Fad or fact? Leadership beliefs and behaviors that emerge. Some ideas pass as fads and others stick as factual ways be better leaders. The fads of Theory X (dictatorial) and Theory Y (touchy-feely) morphed into the fact of Theory Z (situational leadership).

Servant Leadership is gaining momentum after being incubated for several decades. But what's new for leadership now?

Hint: *"As we look ahead into the next century, leaders will be those who empower others."* – Bill Gates, Microsoft co-founder

Five trends in successful leadership

New movements in leadership that include: believing is seeing; empowerment energizes productivity; integral thinking expands opportunity; simplification outruns complexity; happy employees create happy customers.

1. Believing is seeing

What do quantum physicists and spiritual teachers agree upon? That what we see and believe in our mind will manifest in reality. It is not the vision of a leader – it is the belief in that vision by a good team that activates actions which realize the dream.

The conscious leader evangelizes an attractive vision and draws in believers. The believers become achievers. The dream becomes visible. Walt Disney's dream was so compelling that it created an entertainment empire, "Where Dreams Come True."

2. Empowerment energizes productivity

If people do not feel free to be creative, to organically improve products and process, and to collaborate easily with others, business will not accelerate.

Give wide permission with some simple rules to employees, and business velocity will increase. Google empowers its people and has unleashed a rush of innovative products. The company's engineers are encouraged to spend 20% of their time working on projects that interest them.

3. Integral thinking expands opportunity

Black-or-white thinking has been central to business culture for centuries. On-or-off, in-or-out, good-or-bad has been our polarized view. Call it dualistic thinking. But non-dual integral thinkers see both – black-and-white, on-and-off, good-and-bad.

Integral thinking leaders: see options and alternatives; know that every one-sided solution is destined to fail; search for win-win solutions; avoid polarity and all-or-nothing thinking; believe that wisdom is "the art of the possible." Tesla creates stunning products from this somewhat "formless" way of thinking.

4. Simplification outruns complexity

When the value of simplicity is clear, focus is placed on creating uncomplicated products and services. Good leaders demand it. They simplify everything possible. Just because something is simple, does not mean that it must have limited functionality. It just needs to be easy to use.

Simplicity has many benefits: greater attraction; rapid adoption; quicker sale; faster production; loyal customers. Apple drove home the value of simple elegance: irresistible design; efficient user interface; easy to install and use, family of compatible products.

5. Happy employees create happy customers

We thought it was marketing, sales, products, services, price, value. These were the things and actions that we thought brought us customers. Advanced leaders know that if they foster happy employees, those workers will develop happy customers.

And, happy customers become loyal customers. And they bring other new customers along with them by reference and recommendation. Southwest airlines made this point clearly for over 30 years of revenue and profit growth.

The bottom lines

Be a renewed leader. Adopt the newer trends in leadership beliefs and behaviors: believing is seeing; empowerment energizes productivity; integral thinking expands opportunity; simplification outruns complexity; happy employees create happy customers. See dreams come true.

Leadership Lesson 9

Gutless leadership: When courage caves

Every day. Another example of cowardly leadership is reported. A major bank manipulates its customers for increased profitability. A pharmaceutical company pushes prices out of range for those who must have the medications. A corporate CEO skews numbers to please shareholders. The entire U.S. economy is nearly destroyed. Ugly.

Employees get blamed, customers are forgotten, executives are paid stratospheric salaries plus big bonuses. And few go to jail.

The media flack dies down, and the same transgressions are repeated a few years later. What's wrong?

Winners and losers

Consider two types of leaders: courageous and gutless.

The courageous are builders. They build up people and organizations, and support all their stakeholders: employees, customers, vendors, their management teams, and their communities. Honest, open, transparent. They are winners.

The gutless are wreckers. They tear down people and organizations, and manipulate stakeholders. Their primary bottom line is only about profits, and their people are expendable. Dishonest, closed, hidden. They are losers.

Gutless and courageous

Contrasting the gutless with the courageous leaders gives great insight into how to be a good leader – and avoid being a poor one. Here is a chance to identify and strengthen some weak leadership qualities:

Gutless are micro-managers because they do not trust others.
Courageous are macro-managers because they effectively delegate with trust.

Gutless do not have empathy for others.
Courageous respect how their employees and others think and feel.

Gutless serve themselves.
Courageous serve others.

Gutless order others around without respect.
Courageous build good followers and empower them.

Gutless are inept at judging character, including their own.
Courageous see good character in others and engage them for success.

Gutless fear change.
Courageous welcome positive change and foster it.

Gutless are arrogant and believe that they know everything.
Courageous are humble and give credit to their people and others.

Gutless lack vision and demand that others blindly follow.
Courageous have a clear vision and attract others to be part of it.

Gutless have an unbalanced life, burn out, and create chaos.

Courageous have good work-life balance and promote it for others

Gutless perform poorly or not at all.
Courageous establish success through proven performance, not promise.

More ...

Gutless are poor communicators and others are left in the dark.
Courageous communicate clearly (spoken, written, listening) with everyone.

Gutless either set muddy expectations, or have no expectations.
Courageous establish and communicate.

Gutless promote themselves.
Courageous promote others.

Gutless blow with the wind and give in too easily from weakness.
Courageous stand for their principles and successfully negotiate from strength.

Gutless choose others who are like themselves.
Courageous chose others who are better than they are.

Gutless are disorganized.
Courageous organize people, programs, and projects.

Gutless over-promise and under-deliver.
Courageous under promise and over deliver.

Gutless order others around without respect.
Courageous build good followers and empower them.

Gutless have fear.

Courageous have faith.

Gutless follow.
Courageous lead.

Clearly, the positive qualities of a courageous leader offer an increased opportunity to build sustainable success for our organizations - far more than the gutless and their poor to non-existent success, both short and long term.

The bottom lines

Do the right thing. Give up negative qualities of Gutless. Adopt the characteristics of Courageous. These abilities can be learned, practiced, and developed. Build great organizations and sustain them. Start leading. Honestly.

Leadership Lesson 10

Leadership and close encounters of the third kind

You didn't plan it. It just happened. You met someone that you did not know in a meeting, or restaurant, or on an airplane. You started a conversation that led to a business idea and connection that you had never considered. It turned out to be a winning concept that birthed a new product. Or company – even an entire industry. What happened?

Various descriptions of these statistically improbable events include words like cosmic, miracle, karma, synchronicity, grace, luck. And "out of the blue." Or "a one-time chance encounter."

Really? What about the effect of your vision?

Mind set

No, not mindset. You have your mind set on an intention, a dream, a vision for something you want to create. You have been thinking about it for some time, but not much is happening. And, you cannot let go of this idea.

Then, it happens. Someone shows up with the exact resources you need to start moving. Or you see a billboard that triggers the "grand strategy" to give life to your dream. Or an email arrives from a new source of funding that you need. Chance?

"When you want something, all the universe conspires in helping you to achieve it." – Paulo Coelho, author of *"The Alchemist"*

It happened when ...

In the late 1800's a failing mechanical inventor met a successful Detroit coal dealer. They formed a company to build inexpensive transportation for the growing masses of people in the United States. Other investors joined and in 1902 prototype automobile was raced at over 90 miles per hour to establish a new land-speed record. 1903 the company was re-incorporated as the Ford Motor Company. Today, Ford produces more than 5 million vehicles with 200,000 employees in 90 facilities worldwide. Henry Ford wanted to build cars and the "cooperating universe" provided a coal dealer with startup funds.

In 1971 three students who met at the University of San Francisco were drawn to start selling high-end coffee beans and equipment. Later, a coffee brewing equipment salesman, Howard Schultz, called on them to sell his equipment. He ultimately joined them as an employee and then in 1987 bought out the three owners. Schultz quickly expanded their few Seattle shops. Today, Starbucks has nearly 25,000 coffee shops throughout the world. An "out of the blue" meeting turned into a fortune.

In 1995 Larry Page had graduated from the University of Michigan. He was considering Stanford University for advanced schooling. A Stanford student, Sergey Brin, was assigned to give Larry, whom he had never met, a tour. Page entered Stanford. In 1996 Page and Brin began working on an Internet search engine originally named BackRub, running on Stanford servers. In 1997 they formed Google. A "chance encounter" with historical results.

It continues

Steve Jobs met Steve Wozniak and Apple was born. Bill Gates met Paul Allen and Microsoft was birthed. Leaders who are open to "chance encounters" attract resources to build great things.

The bottom lines

Dream big. Be aware of "chance" meetings. An inspiring moment may arise. Statistically improbable events can unfold. Driven by destiny, fate, grace, karma, miracle, synchronicity, cosmic energy, grace, divine providence. Or "it came out of the blue." A "one-time chance encounter." An "out of this world" event. Hold on to your vision. The universe is listening.

Leadership Lesson 11

How successful leaders teach motivation

Drudge? Most of us want to do work that we like and be happy doing it. But more than 50% of workers are unhappy with their jobs. This is a challenge for leaders. Question: how do good leaders create workplaces that are productive, interesting, and fun? Hint: one of the strongest traits of strong leaders is their positive outlook. It is contagious.

Without leadership that is uplifting and motivating, employees can adopt some negative attitudes about work: it is too hard, it doesn't matter, nobody cares. Call it "demotivation."

Smart leaders know also that enthusiasm has two players: the external motivator and the internal motivator. What does this really mean?

Motivation is a partnership

Yes, good leaders exude positive attitudes and progressive actions. Business history is heaped with stories of leaders who moved their organizations from startup to stardom along the path of positivity.

Successful leaders also know that their team members have a responsibility to be self-motivated. But, can self-motivation be acquired?

Given the number of motivational authors, speakers, and workshops, we know that self-motivation can be learned.

Learn this

Assuming that employees are doing work that they like, here are some motivational methods that strong leaders exhibit themselves - and teach to their team members:

<u>Work well done is a prerequisite to success.</u> Good ideas are great – good ideas well implemented are foundational to everyone's wellbeing. Work is an opportunity for creative self-expression and satisfaction.

<u>Be happy while working.</u> Short of singing the songs about work from the fabled "Snow White and the Seven Dwarfs" ("Hi Ho, Hi Ho, Its Off to Work We Go" or "Whistle While You Work"), an upbeat attitude makes work seem easier.

<u>Be grateful for good work.</u> It is an opportunity to create good for others – teammates, the organization, customers, vendors, owners, and community. And, it generates income for ourselves and others.

<u>Don't be shy, silent, and suffering.</u> Ask for help when you need it. When employees try to do too much themselves and then fail, it can be defeating and important projects may be delayed.

<u>Work is rarely as difficult as we project.</u> We seem to approach work as being "hard." We communicate "hard work." A more productive approach is to mentally affirm that work is easy, that we enjoy doing it, and that it has good purpose.

<u>Complaining is counterproductive.</u> It takes us down and can cause others to become anxious and depressed. If we have a legitimate issue, then take it to our leaders for resolution. Praising our work has the opposite effect – it lifts us up!

Work is spiritual in nature. When we are motivated to do our best with meaningful work, we feel a sense of accomplishment and satisfaction. We care for others in the process. Soul filled.

One happy place

A recent *Forbes Magazine* article notes that CareerBliss (www.careerbliss.com) is a workplace fulfillment-focused website. CareerBliss selected UnitedHealthcare as the happiest company in which to work for 2016 – based upon an eight-point rating scale.

The bottom lines

"The road to happiness lies in two simple principles: find what it is that interests you and that you can do well, and when you find it put your whole soul into it — every bit of ambition and natural ability you have." – John D. Rockefeller III, industrialist and philanthropist

Leadership Lesson 12

Why hope is dead in business

Heresy! For thousands of years, hope has been held high as a great human ideal. Elaborated by poets and preachers, promoted by authors and speakers, and hung in office posters by business people everywhere. But there is a downside to hanging out in hope. Better stated, hope is not a plan, and hope is not an action.

Businesses of all sizes have died with large doses of hope. The problem has been that being hopeful is not enough. But when mixed with purposeful plans and absolute action, hope lives.

"In reality, hope is the worst of all evils because it prolongs the torments of man." – Friedrich Nietzsche, philosopher, author

Bad for business

Kodak lost focus in the blizzard of digital photography, sitting in hope that the pixels would go away – and that traditional film photography would hold on. Wrong. Traditional airlines, including United and American hoped that the low-cost gnats, such as Southwest, would be doomed. Wrong. Minicomputer producers, e.g., DEC and Prime, were hopeful that PC's were just a fad. Wrong,

They all died in stubborn hope – acquired, merged, and gone, even though some of their names remained. And many other hopefuls have joined them. Solid strategies, positive plans, and active actions were missing in lieu of hope.

This is why hope is dead.

How long in hope?

Here are some business events that are often hoped for:
- A turnaround in sales
- The right strategic partner
- The perfect marketing manager
- An infusion of capital
- The elimination of debt
- A media break that will take us nationally and globally
- To be the number one company in our industry

No strategy, no plan, no action, just hope? Little probability that any of the above kinds of events will happen. Hope is ephemeral. Short lived. And the longer we hang on to hope alone, the worse our situation will become.

Even if we have a strategy and a plan to implement it, if there is no real action, then we are left with little. Hope without action is just, well, hope!

Loop hole

Hope seems to grind away in an endless loop. We hope, nothing happens, we consider doing something about it, but we do not, and then we loop back into hope.

Decide. Once we make a firm decision to take some action, the loop is broken. We can climb out of the deathly "Hole of Hope."

And typically the first action to take is to develop a strategic business plan with specific actions (by specific people) to implement the plan.

In other words ...

Exchange "hope" for some other words and ways of being, thinking, and doing while you take action: holding to a good vision, being authentic, having faith, speaking positively, building a great team, and moving swiftly.

More: cultivating creativity, holding a winning attitude, demonstrating flexibility, seeking good collaborators and partnerships, establishing challenging goals, and celebrating success often.

Oh yes, another sucker word similar to "hope" is "faith." Remember, "Faith without works is dead."

The bottom lines

Hopeless. Where are you holding on to hope? For how long? You are in a death spiral. Break out of the "hope loop" by making a decision to move forward. Build a solid strategic business plan. Implement it with specific action plans and a great team. Everybody get to work.

Leadership Lesson 13

Uncovering major myths about leaders

Don't believe it. Many of the "truths" about great leadership are not true. They are myths, legends, and smoke. So what is wrong with that? The myths can deter potentially good leaders from trying. Conversely, myths might keep a weak leader in place. For too long.

Here are some of the more popular false beliefs about leaders:
- Wired to work 24 X 7
- Get their "hands dirty" at all times
- Have celebrity quality on-stage charisma
- Must be the CEO or top executive
- Are an expert about everything in the business

And, belief in these legends could deter potential leaders from trying. Tragic.

To explain ...

Here are the truths about some major myths that surround leadership:

Myth: leaders are wired to be 24 X 7 "full on."

Fact: strong, durable leaders know that they need time to plan, digest information, and innovate. Good leaders take time to get back in touch with their being, relook at their dreams, plans, actions, and to be innovative. And, they encourage their team members to do the same – time to reflect and to be creative. Avoids burnout, too.

Myth: leaders must get their "hands dirty" at all times.
Fact: leaders who spend all their time with "do lists" do not have enough time to lead. And, if the leader is not as skilled at given tasks as their team members, why bother to do their peoples' work. Employees might feel that they are not trusted. Or, they might ask why is their leader not performing the critical job of leading? Big problem.

Myth: leaders must have celebrity charisma.
Fact: most leaders do not have magnetic personalities. Many well-known leaders have personal quirks, facial imperfections, or some character deficiencies. But they have excellent interpersonal communication skills. Most of all, they have a strong vision and work at achieving it. Their mission engages others. Results count, not charisma.

Myth: leaders have the highest-level titles.
Fact: real leadership is the result of example, action, and success, not a job title. In many cases, great leaders are not the CEO, but act to support the CEO's vision and mission. Some excellent leaders have nobody reporting to them. And, a leader by title-only can damage an organization. Follow the (real) leader.

Myth: leaders must know more than their employees.
Fact: the best leaders employ the best people who have deep knowledge in different areas of the business. Powerful organizations know this and do not want a "know it all" leader. They feel empowered when they can offer their best to a great team. They get to be a part of something good. Including decisions.

The big one

Myth: leaders are born, not made.

Fact: this myth has been around forever, yet has been proven untrue. Perhaps the best explanation is:

"*The most dangerous leadership myth is that leaders are born – that there is a genetic factor to leadership. That's nonsense; in fact, the opposite is true. Leaders are made rather than born.*" – Warren Bennis, leadership professor, author, consultant

The bottom lines

Ignore leadership myths. The truth is that better leaders are paced, stay above too much detail, are not charismatic celebrities, may not be the CEO, and do not know everything. Above all, good leaders are not born. They are developed by ongoing learning and practice. Always.

Leadership Lesson 14

Are you elevating expectations?

Not challenged? Then you are not likely to be motivated, either. If you are a leader, are you setting higher expectations for yourself? If not, you might not be a leader. Really. And, if you are not raising the bar for yourself, you probably are not establishing greater expectations of others. Nor are you teaching others to raise their own bar and be self-motivated. What's wrong?

Organizational attitudes and behaviors start with expectations from leaders. No expectations result in no leader, no organization, no success. Quick death.

"High expectations are the key to everything." – Sam Walton, founder of Walmart.

What are they anyway?

Some confusion here. Expectations are subtly different than – but related to – goals and plans. These words portray specific desired outcomes – frequently a numerical target (quantitative) and sometimes an objective level (qualitative).

But an expectation is the expectancy, anticipation, or presumption of reaching a goal. Clearly stated expectations about attaining goals are critical to high performance organizations, companies, and businesses. A goal without a leader's expectation that it be met is just a, well, goal.

The best leaders set lofty goals and then hold high expectations that the goals will be met. Or exceeded. Then next year the goals and expectations will be elevated. This is how Olympic world records are set. And beaten.

Expectant leaders

Leaders who drive their organizations with expectations have noticeable qualities. They must to be able to motivate their teams. Here are some of their key leadership characteristics:

Trust – be trustworthy with personal integrity, do what they say they will do, trust others, demonstrate integrity and honesty, don't be a people-pleaser.

Thinking – humans think at a rate of 60,000 thoughts per day, with some 70% of thoughts being negative or repetitive; but leaders control their thoughts to stay positive and focused.

Words – spend more time talking about what is positive, powerful, possible; focus on priorities and progress; speak to encourage others.

Bounds – leaders establish limits, set conditions, say "no" when appropriate, avoid burnout, and help others set boundaries.

Connection – listen carefully, pay attention to others, build bonds with others, communicate clearly, ask for feedback.

Empower – get inputs from others, admit not knowing something, ask great questions, let people know that you appreciate and trust them, support others in their work.

Understand – see all the parts of the business, talk with customers, stay in touch with the organization, communicate with vendors, listen a lot.

Expect – set high expectations of themselves; set high expectations of others; teach others to set high expectations of themselves (self-motivation).

These are only a few of good leadership characteristics that help them set expectations effectively. Their teams respect them and respond positively to them. Everyone wins.

Johnson models it

Johnson Controls is number 67 in the Fortune 500 U.S. largest companies, producing automotive parts, electronics, and HVAC equipment for buildings. They utilize a Leadership Expectations Model with their 170,000 employees. The Model "defines the expected behavior of all Johnson Controls employees — and our key business and people processes — in support of our vision, values and goals."

The bottom lines

Great leaders set great goals. And they set high expectations that goals are met. Good leadership qualities help set high expectations for leaders themselves and their teams. Great leaders help others set their own expectations. The result? More self-motivated leaders.

Leadership Lesson 15

Managing fear before it manages you

Fearless leader? Forget it. No business leader is without some form of fear. Fear of lack, loss, limitation, or liability in some form. Not enough capital, losing a major customer, delays in launching a critical product, and owing payment to a large vendor are a few anxiety amplifiers for leaders. Even the best leaders.

Fear freezes action. It cripples creativity, demoralizes teams, and can threaten the survival of good organizations and businesses. Sitting in fear just makes it worse and delays the inevitable: action.

"When thinking won't cure fear, action will." – W. Clement Stone, businessman, author

Facing fear

Admit it – at least to yourself. And sometimes it is good to mention it to another person. A counsellor, a spouse, a trusted friend, a mentor. Dislodge fear.

Rational fear occurs when we are facing physical danger and need to get away from harm. But most fear is based upon past events that are likely no longer relevant. Which is irrational.

Irrational fear can harm us as well. It can cause great emotional and physical stress. Worse, it fuels burnout. We are living in the problem, not the solution. Get real.

Lights, camera, action

How do great leaders deal with fear? Here are some actions that they take:

Don't sit on your greatest asset – get up and get going; lay out a plan of action; establish priorities and milestones; delegate actions to trusted team members; hold frequent progress meetings; turn fear around and win. Fast.

Get rid of the stress – get some exercise, breathe, meditate, rest up; spend some time with family and friends; watch a hilarious movie; keep doing these things to ward off irrational responses to future irrational stress. Prevention.

Do not run away – even if you feel like it; facing fear head-on is the time-tested antidote; remember that during WWII President Franklin Roosevelt said, "The only thing we need to fear is fear itself." True.

Ask for help – most employees are happy to help resolve issues, including big ones; if you show fear, they will become fearful – if you show fearlessness, so will they. Contagious.

Do not broadcast fear – employees are "fear sensitive," and if the they detect it in their leaders, they will become fearful, making things worse; instead, admit a problem and then engage everyone to help solve it. Fearlessly.

Revisit the vision – fear can be the result of losing track of the target – forgetting the vision that propels you and your business; spend time with your vision; re-affirm your path to success. Energizing.

Above all, believe in yourself and in a trusted power-partner. Divine Providence. Everything is going to be OK. OK?

Fearless Ford

Actually, it was Alan Mulally. In 2006 he became the new CEO of Ford Motor. Two years later GM and Chrysler were begging Congress for bailout money to avoid a recessionary bankruptcy. Mulally declined federal alms, fearlessly faced reality, simplified the business, and by 2009 earned a $2.7 billion profit. CNN quoted him, "If this is the reality, what are we going to do about it?" Action.

The bottom lines

Sweating a problem? Don't wait long. Sitting in fear only prolongs the angst and agony. Take action. Affirm your vision. Build a get-well plan and get going. Do not poison your team by showing your fear. Show your fearlessness.

Leadership Lesson 16

Essentialism and the business of less

Quantity. The American mantra. "More is better" drives consumption. Retail consumers want more of everything in terms of quantity. A bigger home, more clothes, too much food. Likewise, a business consumer can seek too much space, surplus employees, and wasted capital. Excess.

Quality. Smart consumers want better instead of more. A high quality automobile (not necessarily higher priced) will drive better, cost less to maintain and operate, and be worth more at the end of its use. The wise business leader acquires fewer but higher quality people, less machinery, and optimum facilities. With essentialism, we know in our soul what is right. Just right.

"It is only with the heart that one can see rightly; what is essential is invisible to the eye."
– Antoine de Saint-Exupery, French writer and aviator

Be an essentialist leader

The fulcrum – balancing point – of essentialism is our sense of what's right in any given situation. Professional and personal. Having common sense drawn from experience, conscious awareness of situations and conditions, a dose of discernment, and a powerful intuition are all components of being an essentialist.

Leading with intention and purpose instead of running on automatic and emotional fluctuations is the path of the essential leader. Driving the dream, holding to the vision, and minimizing interference bring better results. Focus.

Priorities become paramount for the essentialist leader. What is important and what is not? And a penchant for simplicity minimizes the amount of resources needed. Less is better.

The lighter load

Freedom from excess baggage of thought and action creates cultures that nurture the vision and values, innovation, strategy, maturity, wisdom, interaction, communication. And tenacity with flexibility.

Essentialist leaders embody a number of characteristics that are altruistic and outward focused, including:

Creating good for the world – developing quality products and services that build better lives. In some cases, these goods are donated to worthy nonprofits.

Saying "no" – minimizing low-priority resources and actions is to prevent them. Quickly and professionally stopping the unnecessary provides more focus on the important.

Context driven – the purpose (or the "why") of the leader and the organization is the fuel that fires passionate action. And staying on the road to results.

Clarity of action – avoidance of fractured, scattered, and misspent energy. Once focus is lost, the ability to succeed is throttled.

Lust for information – key operating data is always available, timely, and immediately usable. The organization does not fly blind in a flurry.

Soul-Care – an essentialist leader takes some time each day, week, and month to stop, rest, exercise, eat well, meditate, and read uplifting material. No burnout allowed.

Elimination and reorganization – purging out underused, unnecessary material, processes, collaborations. Make more room for the important.

Always be thinking about, "What is essential?" In all matters, it matters.

Oh what a feeling

Toyota long ago instituted what is called "lean manufacturing." Cutting wasted materials, labor, process steps. Eliminating the unnecessary and focusing on the essentials. Toyota led the quality revolution in the auto industry. Now, they are the largest automotive company in the world. Essentialist leaders.

The bottom lines

Get down to the essentials. In our soul we know what is essential in any situation. Eliminate everything but the essential. The result is more focus on what is important. Quality people, processes, and products. Be an essentialist leader. For good.

Leadership Lesson 17

The art and science of a business model pivot

Like basketball. A player pivots by staying in place while turning quickly on one foot to face a different direction with the ball to score. A great metaphor for a business model pivot. Keeping the vision but doing a fast turn to a new strategy for success. "Turn on a dime."

Often, the pivot refers to an entrepreneurial startup that has a great idea, but is challenged to get the business moving. Typically, the dream is good, but the business model is flawed. Correct the model.

Bigger businesses often have the same issue. The dream for a new product is still good, but a disconnected strategy is blocking the potential for success. Pivot time.

Jack be nimble

One notable pivot occurred in the web of social media startups. A company named Odeo entered the podcast network business. But Apple iTunes had other plans for podcasts and rapidly built market share. Odeo looked at a strategic pivot. Text messaging.

Jack Dorsey, a university student, thought of something similar. He had prototyped a unique text messenger in two weeks. He approached Odeo with his prototype idea. Odeo went for Jack's idea, and rebirthed the company as Twitter. A historical pivot.

"Famous pivot stories are often failures but you don't need to fail before you pivot. A pivot is a change of strategy without a change in vision. Whenever entrepreneurs see a new way to achieve their vision - a way to be more successful - they have to remain nimble enough to take it." –Eric Ries, entrepreneur, author

Good for growth

Beyond a desperate search for a fast pivot in a startup, existing companies can swing pivots to build additional products, services, and markets.

Earth Networks reinvented its core business of networked weather information. They expanded into advertising, networked 8,000 weather stations, and created Weatherbug. Available on mobile devices, Weatherbug a top weather information provider.

Phreesia pivoted to go beyond a provider of clipboard-replacing intelligent tablets for doctors. Now they also provide networked services to help medical staffs better handle co-pays and outstanding balance settlements.

Big pivots

Not just for entrepreneurs, business model pivots are essential for large organizations. These bigger companies have "intrepreneurs" – entrepreneurially-minded employees – who dream up and invent new products for growth. Here are some classic examples:

Wrigley – originally a soap salesman, William Wrigley Jr. was giving away free gum. When the gum became more popular than the soap, he began manufacturing his own gum. Today, billions in revenue and a high-identity brand. Chew on that.

Starbucks – Howard Schultz was selling coffee making equipment. After calling on a small coffee house chain became an employee. Later he bought the Seattle small chain and morphed it into Starbucks. Caffeinated.

HP – Hewlett-Packard began as a large provider of electrical testing products. Its classic pivot was to provide an early large scale PC. While continuing its electronic testing business, its PC and printer/scanner operation is much larger. Clicked.

Business model pivots created *PayPal, Nintendo, Avon, Suzuki.* And many more.

The bottom lines

Pivot time? Entrepreneurial startups or large companies both. When the business model needs reexamination for either traction or expansion, take time to do it or risk stagnation. Or failure. In fact, constant evaluation of your business model is a good idea. Get ready to pivot. Quickly.

Leadership Lesson 18

Gratitude is a daily business

Thanksgiving. Why do we cluster gratefulness into one day per year? The fourth Thursday of November. It is a beautiful holiday to remind us of how much good we have in our lives – including our working lives. Successful leaders know that appreciation is a daily matter – and they show it beyond words. No turkey dinner needed.

But thankfulness is not a frequent expression of most people. UC Berkley research notes that only 10% demonstrate gratitude to their coworkers, and a mere 7% to their employer. Disheartening.

"As we express our gratitude, we must never forget that the highest appreciation is not to utter words, but to live by them." – John F. Kennedy, 45th President of the U.S.

Why not?

Given that we have hundreds of reasons to be grateful daily in our business lives, why aren't we?

Negative stuff – many of us have a natural tendency to focus on what we do not like. We are more prone to complain about people and things we dislike, rather than being grateful for what we do like. Out of balance.

Expectations and entitlement – perhaps we are concerned that we are lacking something we don't have, or losing sometime we do have, or limited in some way, or that we are liable for something. Fear rules.

Busy-ness – we can become so occupied with what we are thinking and doing that we lose sight of what good could be occurring at any given time. If we are not on the look for something to be grateful about, we won't be. Unconscious.

Complacency – if we are so settled into our daily groove of good, we forget to appreciate all that is being given to us. Worse, when the flow of nice things slows down or stops, we might jump into complaining or entitlement. Ho hum.

Lack of gratitude keeps us off balance, fuels fear, leaves us unaware, and dulls us.

Antidotes to ingratitude

As leaders, it is always time to turn our internal switch and start looking for things to be grateful about. Not the least of which to be grateful that we are in leadership positions. It is part of our job to take the lead in expressing appreciation on a daily basis.

Thank employees for their good work. Thank customers for their business and loyalty. Thank prospects for their consideration of your offerings. Thank your community for supporting your company, boards for their support, and vendors for their good products. Be grateful to your family and friends who provide their daily love and nurturing to help you through the day.

And, thank what George Washington and others called Divine Providence – the unseen power that enfolds us and everyone around us. After all, the wise founders of the United States imprinted something important on all of our money. "In God we trust."

Write it down

The Journal of Personality and Social Psychology notes that people who keep weekly gratitude journals experience wellbeing and optimism about each coming week. Use a notebook to record things you are grateful about each day. Read it frequently.

The bottom lines

Get grateful. Not just on Thanksgiving Day. Every day. Great leaders thank their employees, boards and advisors, customers, vendors, local communities. Oh, and their families and friends that provide moral support. Keep a gratitude journal. Daily.

Leadership Lesson 19

See how insight helps leaders learn

An "aha moment." An epiphany. Finally seeing something that has been present for some time. Literally in-sight. These often-abrupt ways of seeing things from a new perspective, offer leaders a way to learn valuable new information. Assuming that the leader is willing to see with "new eyes."

This ability to "see inside" people and situations can solve challenging problems, uncover new opportunities, and avoid difficulties. And it helps engage good employees and others, and motivate organizations for success. Through new learning.

"That is what learning is. You suddenly understand something you've understood all your life, but in a new way." – Doris Lessing, Nobel Prize winner for literature

Learn this

Related terms that help understand more about the nature of insight include: intuition, discernment, perception, awareness, understanding, comprehension, appreciation, penetration, acumen, judgment, acuity, vision. And wisdom.

And revelation. When seemingly unrelated information is combined in our awareness, we see the unseen, and have an opportunity to learn something new. And act upon it.

The insightful leader is able to see through foggy issues that obscure progress. So much so that they appear to have mysteriously found a way to success without having to "figure it out." They have grasped an instinctive "out of the blue" solution. ESP-like.

What do they do?

Leaders with good insight are learning about people, conditions, situations from their insightfulness. There are several practices that they consciously do to enhance their power of insight.

One practice is to maintain good self-care in ways that bring about greater states of relaxation and awareness. Because these states enhance insightfulness. Self-care can include: regular exercise, meditation/mindfulness, time with family and friends, prayer, recreation, yoga, good eating habits, relaxing music, keeping a gratitude journal, self-improvement reading and seminars. And many more.

Another practice for greater insight is to find out what employees and others think. The adage, "The more you know, the more you know," is very true. Insight involves synthesizing seemingly disparate information into cohesive understandings. Bill Gates, co-founder of Microsoft, was a master of getting inputs from employees around the global empire of his company. How? He broadcasted his email address to everyone.

What don't they do?

Great leaders have great insight and are, therefore, excellent learners. They also have strong insights and learning about things that they should never do. Why? Because repetitively doing the wrong thing diminishes insightfulness.

They rarely:
- Fail to find solutions that benefit their organization and themselves.
- Miss a chance to admit their mistakes, and to learn and improve from them.
- Quit advocating for what they believe in; their vision, new opportunities, success.

- Stop listening to inputs and ideas from employees and others.
- Become complacent and stop moving forward.
- Refuse to be humble and give credit to their team and others.
- Involve themselves in mindless debates over trivia, wasting time.
- Get into useless and harmful gossip; only the truth matters.
- Say "yes" to everything; "no" is an acceptable and frequent word.
- Give up; they demonstrate positive attitudes and continuous progress.

Bonus: insight also teaches leaders what to avoid.

The bottom lines

Be insightful. Learn from your increasing ability to "see inside" of people and situations. Practice good self-care and Invite inputs from your organization and others to help gain more insight. Be a better leader. Build a better business. Get insight

Leadership Lesson 20

How to strangle your inner critic

"You can't." This is one of the negative chants that our little voice within uses to ruin our business. Our personal business, which then impacts our professional business. How would you feel if an exterior voice keep telling you that you are not enough to be a good leader?

Not smart enough, strong enough, experienced enough, educated enough, young enough, old enough, fast enough, _____ (fill in the blank) enough. Stop.

"Even our worst enemies don't talk about us the way we talk to ourselves. I call this voice the obnoxious roommate living in our head. It feeds on putting us down and strengthening our insecurities and doubts." – Arianna Huffington, co-founder of the Huffington Post, one of Forbes' Most Influential Women in Media

Internal voice

Listen. Our internal voice is the most powerful voice of all. It can be our best cheerleader to success – or the condemning judge that drives us to self-destruction.

We have a choice. We can listen to our inner critic or we can tune into our inner cheerleader.

Psychologists, self-improvement gurus, quantum physicists, and spiritual teachers are telling us increasingly that whatever we persistently hold in our consciousness is what shows up in our lives. So, learn how to muzzle your inner critic. How?

Red flags, green lights

First, immediately recognize when your inner critic has the microphone. We feel down, defeated, and depressed. Hopeless, out of balance, and we want to hide. From ourselves. When these red flags show up, here are some simple ways to tell your inner critic to stop yapping:

- Simply say "no" at the moment you notice that the self-criticism in your head has started up. Then think of something positive about your business abilities.

- Read your most recent resume and notice the many great things that you have accomplished. It is amazing how much of our greatness our inner critic can drown out.

- Listen to business friends when you ask them about your skills, abilities, and qualities. The majority will surprise you when they tell you about your proven capabilities.

- Do something nice for someone else. If we are too busy listening to our negative "stuff," we ignore others. Acts of kindness for others stops the focus on ourselves.

- Be grateful. Write out a gratitude list and note the things for which you are grateful. Keep adding to it until you notice that your negative voice has turned positive.

- Prioritize and balance your workload. Good leaders know that constant work creates burnout, which only amplifies our inner critic. Take some pressure off.

- Compliment yourself each time you do something positive. And give appreciation to your employees and others when they perform well. It is contagious.

Remember: our self-critic is a subtle spokesperson for the greater foe of self-hatred. Stop self-criticism before it turns into self-loathing. It kills leadership and success.

Stay human

After all, by nature we humans do make mistakes. Great leaders make mistakes, too. But they don't beat themselves up – they admit their errors, learn from them, and then improve.

The bottom lines

Muzzle the inner critic. It is debilitating for leaders and others. It can ruin careers and businesses. Learn how to notice that your self-critic is gnawing away at your positive feelings and energy. Use different tools to strangle your inner critic. Quickly.

Leadership Lesson 21

Don't forget to open the gift of receptivity

Trash it? An unopened gift? Most of us might throw out a gift we have already opened. But unlikely that we would toss one that is still wrapped. Yet many business leaders do it every day. Ignoring valid input, not heeding important warnings, failing to listen to an employee. What's wrong? No receptivity.

Information is a gift. After we receive it, we can choose what to do with it. But failure to even acknowledge the information can be disastrous. Opportunities lost, employees demoralized, customers gone to competitors.

"What helps me go forward is that I stay receptive; I feel that anything can happen."
Anouk Aimee – French actress

Unwrapping the gift

Receptivity has several nuanced meanings: the quality of receiving, taking in or admitting; quick to receive knowledge and ideas; inclined to receive suggestions, offers, and more. Favorably.

Good leaders understand. They have receptive minds and are receptive listeners. And readers, too. They even solicit, welcome, and are grateful for inputs.

Bill Gates, co-founder of Microsoft, was receptive to ideas from his team. He invited employees globally to provide their inputs. How? He gave his email address to them, had his staff gather up their emails and consolidate the information. Gates knew a lot about what was happening around the company. He opened the gift of vital information. With gratitude.

Tune in

How can leaders and others be more receptive? Here are some proven practices:

Ask – make it clear that you want inputs. And you can clarify how you would like to receive it: face-to-face, email, phone call.

Meet – hold periodic meetings with randomly selected employees, ask for their inputs, and listen. Ask some specific questions and hear their answers.

Qualify – tell inputters that if they complain, then they must include a proposed solution. If they are chronic complainers without solutions, don't listen any more.

Participation – when good employees describe specific problem areas, ask them if they will participate in finding a solution. Perhaps as part of a team.

Engage – if someone has a good idea that is worth pursing, invite them to take a lead in implementing the idea (assuming they have the capability). Give them resources.

Read – good leaders are good readers. They absorb appropriate emails, books, and articles. They spot trends in their company – and the industry, products, and people.

Conferences – along with seminars, are sources of good information about how to be a better leader. Education.

Listen up

Receptivity involves active listening. So much of our daily input is verbal. Strong leaders listen more and talk less. A *Harvard Business Review* article suggests that we should listen ten times more than we talk. The more we learn the better. Even if we listen twice as much as we talk, a Talk/Listen Ratio of 2:1, we are the gainers.

If we do not focus on what someone else is saying we miss an opportunity to be receptive, to learn, to be involved deeply, to show respect. And, to be respected.

We only learn from ourselves when we talk incessantly, but we learn from others when we listen attentively.

The bottom lines

Open it. The gift of receptivity. Information can mean better leadership, better organizations, better products and services. Ask for information and absorb it. Failure to receive facts willingly can mean failure. Fatal.

Leadership Lesson 22

Out with stagnation, in with reinvention

Change. It is a constant in business. Failure to change our business and ourselves as leaders is a dead end. Why? Because everything else around us is changing. Markets move, technologies evolve, processes improve. Leadership principles and practices elevate. Stand still amidst change and you stagnate.

Or reinvent and move ahead. Not just once a year. Anytime. Better yet, all the time. Especially in the high-velocity of business today. Change to win.

"People who cannot invont and reinvent themselves must be content with borrowed postures, secondhand ideas, fitting in instead of standing out." – Warren Bennis, leadership author and professor

Smart change

In order to make effective change, know what to change. How? Turn your radar on and scan everything that is happening in the organization, the business, the company, the markets, competition, the industry. Where are the trends? Ride the trends quickly.

Inside the company, discover where the issues and opportunities lie. Where are changes needed? Plan and implement modifications or entirely new ways of doing business. Soon.

Look at your leadership style. How do you need to adapt to an ever-shifting workforce and work environment? Find mentors and others who can help you change. To the new and improved leader.

Company reinvented

IBM. The "think" company. By 1984 IBM owned the PC market. Their open systems approach both built their market dominance – and then destroyed it. PC clones overwhelmed the market and IBM was largely shut out. By 1994 IBM suffered one of the greatest corporate losses ever. $8 billion. They sold the PC business and reinvented the company as an IT services giant. Out with the old, in with the new.

Leadership reinvented

Apple. The "think differently" company. Steve Jobs reinvented a stream of stylish products. And he reinvented leadership. Driven by authenticity and passion, he incorporated a personal style with black turtlenecks, developed a charismatic manner, produced surprise, and pitched the positive side of failure. Paradoxically, he spoke to the finite nature of life and living it. Just before he died at age 56.

The art and science of reinvention

Once you have decided to stop sitting in stagnation, and step into success – game on! Here are some ideas to help the process of reinventing your organization. And yourself.

Understand – what you do want, what you don't want, and why. Move toward your vision of the new business and you as a new leader. When success arrives, you will know it and like it.

Commit – you do not have to justify your reinvention to anyone. Just speak your truth simply and keep moving. The few minutes of someone else's opinions are not worth you having to spend years in stagnation.

Search – for others who will help you. Business mentors and coaches who have been through reinventions of organizations, companies, and leaders. Interestingly, an increasing number of leaders want reinvention.

Act – planning for reinvention without actually doing it is just more stagnation. Reorient any fear of risk toward the excitement of new opportunities.

Above all, be honest with yourself and others. It facilitates reinvention.

The bottom lines

Change happens. Whether you like it or not. You can refuse to change and stagnate both your business and your leadership. But reinvent yourself and your organization and you'll have an exciting opportunity for success. A big one.

Leadership Lesson 23

Write your future resume now

20/20 hindsight. That is what nearly all resumes and bios reflect about leaders – and others. But some quantum physicists and spiritual teachers offer a new twist. What we envision in our minds and focus upon is what tends to show up in our lives. Amazingly.

So, why not put your dream into the form of a resume as you would like it to read in a few (or more) years from now? As though it has already happened? Powerful.

"The challenge of life, I have found, is to build a resume that doesn't simply tell a story about what you want to be, but it's a story about who you want to be." – Oprah Winfrey, businesswoman, entertainer, philanthropist

Start writing now

How? Spend some time thinking about your dream leadership role. Picture what you would like to have in three to five years and write about it:

- Begin writing by taking your existing resume as a starting point. Use a resume format that feels right for you.

- Add into the beginning of your new resume a vivid description of your ideal leadership role as though you have already accomplished it. Describe it in vivid detail.

- Include some emotions you feel as the result of succeeding in your advanced career step as a great leader. Write about those emotions.

- Incorporate some data that show your ability to reach measurable goals. Your goals should be attainable, relevant, and time-bound – and include some numerical results.

- Be specific about what kind of leadership role you will have held. Include the industry, company (actual or example), and your responsibilities.

- Outline your desired qualities as a leader: purpose, values, interpersonal skills, leadership characteristics, measures of personal success.

- List the leadership skills, personality makeup, outside interests, and work experience that you will have had in order to succeed in your future leadership role.

When you have created your future resume, ask some friends who know you well to critique your draft. Do not ignore them. Listen to their inputs and make appropriate improvements to your document.

Now what?

Read it often. With feelings of success. The act of focusing on your desired future will help intensify and enliven your dream. The more you read and reflect about your envisioned resume, the more likely that it will come true.

This is why great athletes also practice their games in their minds – in addition to live practices. This has been proven for decades.

When your future resume is well written, you might use it to look for a new career step or job. Someone interviewing you could well be impressed and be able to see you in a new leadership role. One that you would like to have!

The Disney Dream

Walt Disney believed in his dream of being a commercial artist and entertaining the world. He won 22 Oscars and 7 Emmy's. He became a founder and leader of the entertainment empire, The Walt Disney Company. He wrote his future resume in his head and on his sketch pad.

The bottom lines

A dream resume. Write yours now. What leadership role would you like to have in three to five years? Envision it and write it in great detail. Literally. Read it often because it is your roadmap to realizing your dream. Don't settle for less.

Leadership Lesson 24

Watch out, here comes "neuro-leadership"

What? Is this the latest faddy buzz in leadership theory? Maybe. And maybe not. Neuroleadership has caught the keyboard of *Harvard Business Review* writers and others. Based upon new brain-based research, one of neuro-leadership's key benefits is its contribution to effective collaboration. There is more.

Neuroscience in brain research is influenced by medicine, physics, pharmacology, and psychology. And, neuroscience influences neuro-education, neuro-law, neuro-ethics. And now neuro-leadership.

"Progress depends on our brain. The most important part of our brain, that which is neocortical, must be used to help others and not just to make discoveries." – Rita Levi-Montalcini, Italian neurobiologist, Nobel Prize winner

The application

The ability to better understand the workings of the human brain has led to discoveries about how we react or respond to different situations and conditions. Thanks to psychology.

Because organizational behavior is related to psychology, neuroscience is getting noticed in business. Human Resources in particular is now tuning into the possibilities of neuroscience having a positive impact on individuals and groups in business.

Dr. David Rock, involved in developing neuroscience in leadership, adopted the term "neuroleadership" and developed trainings for its applied use in business. He leads the Neuroleadership Institute. www.neuroleadership.com

What does it do?

At the highest level, neuroscience is a "brain-based model for collaborating with and influencing others." Dr. Rock names his model as SCARF – to define our human experiences with status, certainty, autonomy, relatedness, and fairness.

We can respond to these areas with feelings of a pending reward – or react as if there is a perception of a threat. Either way.

One interesting idea is that most people are naturally motivated in the workplace – and the job of the leader is to create cultures, values, and behaviors that avoid demotivating already-motivated employees. Such as top-down autocratic management styles.

Putting it to use

Periodic performance appraisals of employees can be threatening and demotivating. A former HR director of Merrill Lynch notes that this kind of feedback can go badly – even when it is well constructed and delivered.

Juniper Networks in the U.S. has moved away from the traditional appraisal method to a conversational process involving employees, their peers, and even customers. This process looks forward for the employee, rather than backwards.

An employee survey found: 88% saw an increase in engagement among their colleagues; 76% noted their peers were better positioned for positive change.

What else?

More usage of neuroleadership in corporations has offered:

Greater collaboration – in learning and application because of enhanced insight and intuition.

Memory improvement – visual and spatial memory due to improved morale and employees staying in their jobs for longer periods of time.

Adaptation to change – neuroleadership applied to large-scale organizational changes helped employees better understand the changes and adapt more easily to them.

Stress management – better decision making, greater effectiveness in dealing with employee issues.

Better HR programs – when HR designs new programs and processes using neuroleadership tools, the programs are more acceptable and effective.

The *Wall Street Journal* and *Harvard Business Review* continue to provide articles about neuroleadership. Something to consider in business organizations.

The bottom lines

Neuroscience is new. Neuroleadership is even newer. It has early successes with leadership styles that improve collaboration, training, and morale. Its corporate advocates have jettisoned conventional employee evaluations. Why? Performance improves with new collaborative peer evaluations. Watch for neuroleadership.

Leadership Lesson 25

Dump dumb goals and get SMART

Vague? Worse, unwritten? We are talking goals. Per a Harvard University study, 83% of our population have no goals, 14% have some mental goals, and only 3% have written goals. Harvard also discovered that their MBA graduates who had clearly written goals earned ten times more than those without documented goals. Seriously.

Mushy goals are not goals. They lack definition, have no means of knowing whether they are ever completed, are not assigned to anyone, are unrealistic, and have no defined ending. Why bother?

"A dream becomes a goal when action is taken toward its achievement." – Bo Bennett, businessman, professor, author

A smarter way

SMART is an effective goal-setting method often associated with management guru Peter Drucker's teachings about "management by objectives." SMART stands for the five components of a well-set goal: Specific, Measurable, Achievable, Realistic, Time-bound:

Specific

The question is specific to what? If it is sales, which segment of sales. What volumes for what products. In what geographies. A sales goal might be written as, "We will sell 5,000 units of our ABC system in the U.S. the first quarter, and increase it by 1,000 units for the next three quarters. Our VP of Sales is accountable for meeting this goal."

Measurable

Can the goal be measured easily in a meaningful, numerical manner? How many employees will be hired. How many units will be produced. Define the speed of the new product. Once this metric is established, then progress can be tracked. "We will engineer this motor turn at a constant 5,000 RPM's under a load of 2,000 pounds."

Achievable

Can the goal actually be met? If it cannot be attained reasonably, it is self-defeating and potentially demoralizing. Yes, goals should be challenging, but set the target so that it is possible to reach it. Test the reasonableness of the goal with your team. "Our manufacturing team has agreed to increase production by 25% this year."

Realistic

Does the goal support the overall purpose, vision, values, mission, and strategy of the company? If not, find another goal. Every goal should be tested against the key driving factors of the business. Unrealistic goals can damage the organization. "While we are in the garment business, we will now compete in the food industry." Seems irrational.

Time-bound

When will this goal be completed? The year, month, day must be defined for every goal. Likewise, lay out the milestone dates along the way (with SMART). Time adds a sense of urgency and teamwork, progress can be tracked, wins celebrated. "We will launch this new marketing campaign this coming October 1, first testing it by August 31."

SMART is a proven way to accelerate the growth and success of the business. And don't forget to document all goals and review them. Frequently.

SMART example

"We will achieve our sales goal of 1,000 green XYZ systems in the first quarter of this coming year, increased by 15% in each of the following three quarters by launching a weekly marketing campaign on January 1, and by hiring one new sales person at the beginning of each quarter."

The bottom lines

Get SMART. Dump vague, unwritten goals. Harvard University and others have proven the significant value of goals that have five clear components: Specific, Measurable, Achievable, Realistic, Time-bound. Write them and track them. Succeed.

Leadership Lesson 26

Here are assumptions that will kill your business

Wait. You had a stellar business model all figured out. Rich with possibilities for the future and your team loved it. But when it was implemented, it did not meet the intended goals. The revenue stream was choked off, profits suffocated, and the death of the company was imminent. What happened?

Here is a clue from a dictionary: "Assumption – a thing that is accepted as true or as certain to happen, without proof." Unfortunately, we tend to believe that our assumptions are true. Bad idea.

"Assumptions are the termites of businesses." – Anon

Tired

Firestone Rubber Company had enjoyed being at the top of U.S. tire manufacturers for decades. Harvey Firestone Sr., founder, was friends with the leaders of the U.S. automotive industry. The Firestone company culture was unified, loved by employees, and was seen as an all-American corporation.

The company was well-aware that the newer radial tires were gaining traction in Europe in the 1960's. In the 1970's, Firestone made its move and invested in radial production. But by 1979, the company's business had gone flat and worse. Its formerly fully-loaded factories were running at only 59% of capacity. Firestone refused to close plants, bore huge losses, and was ultimately acquired by Bridgestone Tire.

What went wrong? Firestone made two fatal assumptions: one, that demand for their products would enjoy continuous growth; two, that radial tires could be produced in the same manner as conventional tires. Both wrong. And fatal.

Killer assumptions

OK, so we do need to make some assumptions about the future: markets, products, sales, services, customer support, collaborations and strategic partnerships, the economy, production, costs. And more. The question for each assumption is, "How realistic is it?" Here are some danger areas to avoid about assumptions:

Basing assumptions only upon the past – yes, we do need to factor in the past, but not paying attention to future trends and breakthrough ideas is bad. Think about all angles.

Not validating assumptions with others – forming our assumptions alone can be a flawed ego trek. Ask team members and smart outsiders. More validation is better.

Believing there is no competition – a classic, insane assumption. Even if you cannot see them yet, better to believe that if you have a good idea, someone else will try to beat it.

Thinking that your customers are loyal – when good customers find a significantly better value, they will wave good bye. Keep putting better value in front of them. Always.

Skipping perceived low-value functions – e.g., forget marketing and just sell more; don't train employees because they have had enough. These flaws are insidious. And costly.

Assuming that the team is strong – believing that no key players will leave. Worse, thinking none should be asked to leave. Get ready to shut the business down. Soon.

Presuming the economy will improve – this has two sides: that the bad economy will get better right away; that the good economy will get better forever. Time to adjust to reality.

The worst assumption of all? We don't have any problems. Death wish.

The bottom lines

Assume anything. But don't believe it until you test it against reality with others. And then don't believe them completely. Use assumptions when necessary. Test them repeatedly. Be prepared to change them quickly. Bad assumptions can kill good businesses.

Leadership Lesson 27

This is how to defy uncertainty

Oh, no. Just when you think everything is cool, it isn't. A big upset. An important new product failing after shipment. A massive production run gone bad. A huge order unexpectedly lost to competition. No amount of planning would have prevented it. Now you do not know what to do about it. Hello, uncertainty. But how can we learn to live with it? Read on.

Yes, there are upside surprises and they are much better, right? Maybe. What if you had won the huge order instead of losing it to the competitor. And then found out that you do not have the production capacity and raw materials to fulfill the order.

"Uncertainty is a permanent part of the leadership landscape. It never goes away." – Andy Stanley, minister

Prevent, minimize, and remediate

Ignoring uncertainty won't make it evaporate. But creative, concerted action will help manage it. There are a couple of conscientious choices we can make. One is to prevent as much uncertainty as possible. Two, minimize the effects of unplanned events. And three, remediate the aftermath of those unfortunate happenings that could not be prevented (or were not prevented).

Prevention
Right. We cannot prevent every damaging event. But we can anticipate many. Welcome to risk management. Find a full-time or part-time strong person to take it on. Their role is to work alone and with teams to outline every conceivable area in the organization that could go wrong. Then outline actions to prevent as many unfortunate events as possible. With full support from the leaders of the organization. And complete awareness of priorities, impacts, and costs. Prevent fires.

Minimize
OK, if an undesired occurrence cannot be completely prevented, perhaps it can be contained in a way to lessen its effects. Use the list developed for "Prevention," above, and decide in advance what actions will be taken to minimize the damage. Put processes in place that people will follow to dampen a bad situation. Fight fires.

Remediate
Worst case. A disaster happens and it could not have been prevented nor minimized. Now what? Have a plan in place to repair the situation as quickly and efficiently as possible. Knowing ahead of time can save time and cost – and sometimes stop the spread of the damage. Clean up after the fire.

The greatest damage done from events that are born out of uncertainty is to do nothing about them – before, during, or after.

What could go wrong?

Oh, anything. Physical damages to facilities and equipment; loss of good employees; losing orders that were "in the bag;" an expensive production facility that fails; new technology that has random, intermittent failures; an expensive marketing campaign that gets no traction; a large batch of flawed raw material from a single-source supplier; a surprising financial loss; unexpected damaging legislation; a gorilla of a new competitor with a far better product at a much lower cost; another recession. Ad nauseam.

List all possibilities and look for ways to prevent, minimize, and remediate as an ongoing business activity.

Before it is too late.

The bottom lines

Deal with uncertainty. It is all around our businesses all the time. Prepare for it through planned prevention. Use known ways to minimize the effects of unplanned events. Define ways to cleanup damage from undesired situations. Before it happens.

Leadership Lesson 28

The tyranny of vagueness

Maybe. Sort of. Perhaps. All vague terms that we live with daily. Might be sometimes ok in our personal lives. Not good in our business lives which depend upon an obsession with accuracy. Or as much accuracy as we can muster. The problem is that vagueness is easy - and factual accuracy is often difficult. And so we avoid accuracy.

Vagueness is similar to assumptions. When we believe our assumptions to be true, we are in murky water. When we believe our vague statements and "facts" to be true, we are tyrannizing ourselves and our businesses. Danger.

"The changing of a vague difficulty into a specific, concrete form is a very essential element in thinking." - J. P. Morgan, American businessman and banker

Fuzzy focus

Conglomerates were popular collections of unrelated companies via mass acquisitions. Their businesses were widely varied. For example, one of them sold textiles, military aircraft, and many other kin-less products. They existed because of low interest rates that supported acquisitions - and oscillating bear and bull markets that were conducive to leveraged buyouts. High flyers.

Remember Ling-Temco-Vought (LTV), ITT, Litton, Textron, Teledyne pre-year 2000? All are gone. When interest rates later rose, the high-flying conglomerates crashed. Fast.

The conglomerates were a challenge to absorb and manage the myriad acquisitions. And vague visions, missions, strategies, and intended actions did not help. Entanglement.

When the critical factors of business are vague, chaos grows. Vagueness translates to ambiguity and confusion. The entire business is at risk and can accelerate an unnecessary death of a potentially great company. Clearly, something needs to be done to replace vagueness. What?

Communications clarity

The tyranny of vagueness starts with poor communications. About anything and everything. If any form of communications is vague, the message is messy. No matter what form of communication: spoken, written, read, or heard. When the intended audience (even if one person) does not grasp the meaning of the message, it is lost. Sometimes with serious implications.

Sometimes the worst communication is no communication. When an organization does not know the rudimentary purpose and direction of the business, how can they trust the leadership and do their best to support success?

Lack of clear communications creates a condition where anything can happen, everything can happen, or nothing can happen. So, how can we as leaders (and others) build better ways to communicate – everything?

The lens of clarity

Be clear. Here are some simple steps leaders, managers, and others can take to increase clarity and decrease vagueness. In any kind of communications: spoken, written, text, email, face-to-face, phone call, or video communications:

Purpose – it helps to describe the reason for our communications. What is the message about? Why is it being communicated now? How does it relate to the business?

Check – when communicating, ask the recipients, "Is this clear? What about it is not clear? How could we make it more clear?"

Tell – if you are the communication recipient and do not understand, say so. Just ask, "Would you please clarify that for me?"

Clear communications should be with anyone: employees, vendors, customers, collaborators, and the market. Everyone.

The bottom lines

End the tyranny of vagueness. Get clear. Ask questions to clarify all communications. Build clarity into the organization's values and culture. Everyone should embrace it. Vagueness kills, clarity heals.

Leadership Lesson 29

Women, leaders, and sledgehammers on the ceiling

Cleopatra? Curie? Thatcher? Sure, women have been great social leaders, teachers, and scientists. But as business leaders in the "man caves" of executive lairs? Cracking the glass ceilings of prominence and pay scales? Slow start. But shift is happening.

New stats: 36% of the 2015 U.S. top business school enrollees are women (including Harvard and Wharton), up from 32% in 2011 – make that 40% at Stanford in 2017. Oh, now more women than men are expected to earn undergraduate degrees in business.

Too, in 2013 there were 20 women CEOs of Fortune 500 companies – and a year later 24. Their corporations include: General Motors, Hewlett-Packard, IBM, Pepsi, Lockheed Martin, DuPont, Duke Energy, Gannett. And, women hold 20% of S&P company board seats. More to come. Why?

Vive la difference

Research by Utah Valley University and others found some common aspects of women leaders:

Families – fathers in particular encouraged discussions about politics, business, and social matters. Girls' curiosity and eventual involvement is promoted.

Education – advanced schooling is supported by families and others. It became the rule, rather than the exception, for young women to graduate with university degrees.

Organic – men are on a strategic path to leadership. Women are experiential and organic on the road to leadership - motherhood, nonprofits, and boards pave the way.

Diverse – women aggregate many experiences of management from family to the grocer to the banker to the PTA. They turn these into a rich set of leadership skills.

Standards – women tend to be held to higher standards than men. And women set high standards for themselves to overcome biases toward their ability to lead.

Instincts – when it comes to intuition and insights, women have more natural tendencies than men toward these "touchy-feely, spiritual" leadership abilities. Some men strive for them.

Competitive – women believe that they have much to prove in a male-dominated business world. So, they will work long and diligently to succeed in their leadership roles.

Interestingly, Pew Research polls indicate that 44% believe that in time women will hold as many executive roles as men. It is already happening.

Entrepreneurial, too

There are now more than 10 million women-owned businesses in the United States, 35% of all small businesses. And that growth is over 25% per year – faster than men-owned businesses. Don't believe that men are more entrepreneurial than women.

Cars to cosmetics

In 1970, Anita Roddick visited "The Body Shop" in Berkeley, CA. It was a former car repair shop, converted to a cosmetic store. In 1976, she opened a similar shop in England and paid the Berkeley shop owners $3.5 million for the name. She built a culture of environmentally safe products, self-esteem for women, and philanthropy.

Anita's shops expanded at 50% per year and in 2006 she sold the business to L'Oréal, the French cosmetics giant, for $950 million. Today, The Body Shop has over 2,600 stores globally.

In 2007, Anita Roddick died of a cerebral hemorrhage. One of her memorable quotes is, *"If you think you're too small to have an impact, try sleeping with a mosquito."*

The bottom lines

The "glass ceiling" is cracking. Women business leaders are increasing at all levels: large corporations and small-medium businesses. CEO roles, board positions, and women-owned companies. Women are well-educated, instinctive, hold high standards, and work painstakingly. Success!

Leadership Lesson 30

Don't sit on it – standup for fast progress

Sitting. Most of us sit on our greatest asset, including meetings. But there are several drawbacks to sit-down meetings – especially when tracking tight-timeline programs. The meetings become unnecessarily long and fail to stay point. Worse, key projects can go off track. Costly.

Standup meetings are increasingly popular. Standing forces shorter, to-the-point sessions. Leaders see key projects moving forward at a faster pace. Participants enjoy short, crisp meetings. More time to get the important things done. Successfully.

"The human body has two ends on it: one to create with and one to sit on. Sometimes people get their ends reversed. When this happens, they need a kick in the seat of the pants." – Theodore Roosevelt, 26th President of the United States

Standup, scrum, and Kanban

Borrowed from the sport of rugby, a precursor to U.S. style football, the scrum is preparation for action. The players stand up, gather together, take their places, assess the situation, and prepare for more action – a great metaphor and another name for fast standup meetings. Kanban emanated out of Toyota's lean production processes.

Call it a standup meeting, or a scrum, or a Kanban. Same thing. While the origins of these highly focused and brief meetings were in IT, they now apply across the board. In project management, knowledge working, lean production, agile software development.

Standups in knowledge working can embrace faster-paced progress in HR, marketing, organizational development, accounts payable and receivable, executive leadership, and other areas. Amazing!

Do it yourself kit

Here are 12 proven methods to use in your own standup meetings:

1. Hold them daily at the same time and in the same place. Consistency matters.
2. Everyone stands up during the entire meeting. It commands attention.
3. Appoint a competent facilitator. Someone has to keep the meeting on track.
4. Limit the meeting to between 5 and 15 minutes. This maintains focus.
5. Do not postpone a meeting if some of the participants cannot attend. Keep moving.
6. The meeting is for the team to make progress a project. Not to inform management.
7. Limit the scope of the project so it can be addressed within 15 minutes. No more.
8. Keep the size of the presenting team to no more than 15 people. Speed counts.
9. Each member reports progress, completions, obstacles. In about 1 minute.
10. Other members can say, "See me afterward for some help." It is a team effort.
11. Use a computer-based project management tool (e.g., JIRA). The team updates it.
12. Project the updated management tool at the meeting for all speakers. More clarity.

And, consider having a key leader sit in on one meeting each week to see progress, make suggestions – and applaud the team!

Why bother?

Daily standup meetings provide many benefits: builds strong, organic teams; prevents problems from ballooning; promotes focused follow-up conversations offline instead of in the meetings; creates bonds among the team members. Most of all, faster, more accurate progress in key projects. Ask Apple and Google why they use standups. Proof.

The bottom lines

Get off of it. Start holding daily 15-minute standup meetings to accelerate the progress of your critical projects. Use the above 12 methods to drive your standups. Save time, get faster, more accurate results, stronger teams. Don't sit on it. Standup now.

Leadership Lesson 31

Ending the terminal uniqueness of "no competition"

Not one? No competitors, you say. You might be unique – terminally unique. Another look at the farmland of innovation and entrepreneurship will tell you if there is anything else growing out there. Or not. In either case, you might be living in self-delusion.

If you are first to market with your stunning new idea and do not have a competitor, worry. For two reasons: either you will have a beastly challenger soon, or your idea is not worth competing against. Huh?

"I have been up against tough competition all my life. I wouldn't know how to get along without it." – Walt Disney, entrepreneur, animator, film producer.

Been and has been

The graveyard of once-great companies that ignored or didn't believe that they had competition is full. Here are a few headstones:

Netscape – they started the search engine roar at the beginning of the Internet races. They grabbed market share quickly. Then Microsoft got on the track with Internet Explorer and took 95% of the market away. Until Google appeared.

Kodak – the U.S. king of cameras, film, and film processing. They stayed in the darkroom and did not look at a bigger picture of the emerging digital photography age. Canon, Sony, and others did. In 2012 Kodak filed bankruptcy and the "Kodak Moment" was over.

American Airlines – this Dallas-based carrier enjoyed decades of high-flying growth. Years later another airline was Dallas-born and ignored. Until Southwest Airlines became a major reason for American's death – and rebirth as a merged company.

There are more: Blackberry vs. Apple iPhone, IBM PC vs. HP and Dell, General Motors vs. Toyota. Ever hear of Blockbuster video rentals?

Nobody loves me

You have launched a fantastic product (according to you). You brag that you have no competition – and you are right. Why not?

1. Nobody wants your product. You have an issue (unknown to you) with features, price, how it is marketed – worse, it solves a problem that the intended buyer does not have. Potential competitors know this and are staying away.

2. You misread your market. You might have a good business idea, yet you are not seeing competitors in your segment. There may be competitors who are satisfying your intended customers with a partial solution in a different manner.

3. Your market isn't ready. And there can be many reasons. Potential customers might like what you have, but they are not ready to change. Or your product does not quite fit their need. And they might be waiting to see if there are any competitors. Yet.

No might be an opportunity to tune your product-market fit and offer a winning solution.

Treasure hunt

Want to find out more about your competitors? Try these tips: start asking industry experts who know them; establish alerts on search engines to get competitor news; visit them at trade conferences; witness their presentations; look at their websites; talk with their customers. Don't copy your competitors – do more for your customers.

The bottom lines

No competitors? Trouble. Look for them, because if you do not see them now, you will. Soon. Worse, if you do not see them soon, why not? Perhaps because no customers or competitors value what you are selling. Bragging that you do not have any competitors is a business disease named "Terminal Uniqueness." Fix it fast.

Leadership Lesson 32

Your disruptive consciousness drives a new business era

Disruption. Where does it start in business? Something within us, our consciousness, is the receiving dock for "out of the blue, aha moments." Our inner pulses that drive new ideas. The kind that tip over an entire industry – or world. And birth hundreds of new businesses. And jobs.

Consciousness is ascending as a core business component. It is the high ground of life, including business. It is coming into focus with existing businesses, plus universities, quantum physicists, spiritual teachers, and corporate leaders.

It promotes entrepreneurship, competition, freedom of trade, trust, compassion, collaboration and value creation. And it is focused on serving the better interests of all stakeholders: customers, employees, owners, vendors. And the global community.

Who started it?

Credit is given to Anita Roddick for igniting the conscious business advance. She founded The Body Shop in 1976 and promoted successfully the ideas of environmental protection, sustainability, human and animal rights. And major philanthropy.

Others, including the leaders of Nordstrom's, Trader Joe's, and The Container Store joined in. More recently Howard Schultz, CEO of Starbucks, joined the conscious commerce movement.

USA Today ran a story about the growing wave of millennials who embrace conscious business – supporting beneficial business practices throughout the world.

Elevator up

A hardened hierarchy of business is ascending into higher states of consciousness. The bottom levels of scary and depressing commerce environments are rising to higher levels of harmonious and hopeful domains.

So we are taking the express elevator up Maslow's pyramid of human needs – from the basement of survival to the penthouse of well-being for all stakeholders.

"The key to growth is the introduction of higher dimensions of consciousness into our awareness." – Lao Tzu, Chinese philosopher and writer

Milestones of the movement

As this trend of higher consciousness in business accelerates, there are progress indicators to watch for. Here are a few:

- Big fairness to customers, employees and others is more important than big data.

- "We" replaces "me" – new Gen's are more interested in humanity than the next dollar.

- "Only one way" gives way to "many ways" – infinite options abound.

- Painting dreams in our consciousness with positive emotions produces great results.

- Global coexists with national and local commerce – customers anytime, anywhere.

- Collaborative leadership supersedes vertical management – more success for all.

- Strategy and tactics intertwine and flow together at all times for smoother progress.

- High-speed, pervasive communications spreads compassionate commerce.

Making life overrides making money. Business leaders of a higher consciousness create organizations to build a prosperous world that works for an increasing number of people. And they give some of their profits away. For decades, Target Corporation has given 5% of their profits to community causes. Currently $4 million per week to resolve hunger, help disaster relief, support the arts, and assist youth in completing high school.

Providence and trust

There is an acknowledgement of a spiritual aspect to conscious business. George Washington called it, "Divine Providence." He and his co-founders of the United States printed something unique on all of our money: "In God We Trust." It has worked very well for over 200 years. In spite of periodic cycles of distrust.

The bottom lines

Elevate your business consciousness. Build and support organizations that foster fairness, entrepreneurship, trust, compassion, collaboration, and value creation. Make money and make better lives. For everyone.

Leadership Lesson 33

Goodbye networking, hello connecting, and 5 ways to do it

Connecting vs. networking? You mean there is a difference? Definitely. Going to networking meetings, quickly meeting a bunch of people, and being a packrat for business cards is passé. In connecting, quality beats quantity. Depth is the difference.

"Connectors" are those who value meeting new people, getting to know them, building meaningful relationships, and offering to be helpful. This is the ascendant realm of great leaders. Meaningful matters.

"A very simple concept that goes back 50 million years; it's about leading and connecting people and ideas. And it's something that people have wanted forever." – Seth Godin, American author, entrepreneur, and marketer

Meet the connector

They are members of a community who have a large number of professional and personal contacts. Connectors are a hub – at the center of a socio-business exchange. They willingly make introductions of people in the same circle, and people of differing circles. They want to help others.

Connectors know people from diverse circles – professional, social, cultural, and economic clusters of like-minded interests and abilities. They have an "inner radar" that can match the right people for the right reason.

They have a passion and skill to bring the right people together for the better interests of all. If they had a motto it would be, "Bringing people together for something good." Their skill is building friendships and making meaningful introductions.

Starter kit

Leaders who are strong connectors value the "why" of building a number of significant business relationships. Important ideas and information is exchanged. Greater, powerful resources become available. And there is a larger opportunity to help others.

An important book by author Lynne McTaggart, *The Bond*, provides plenty of proof that we humans are inherently wired to help each other. During our careers, most of us have experienced growth by being connected with others who helped us. We might have given an important new career step. Just one example.

And now we recognize the value in helping others – by connecting them with others.

5 ways of the effective connector

Here are the key tenets of successful leaders who are connectors:

1. Be a friend – when meeting new people listen a lot, and talk some. Share your career and personal stories. Get to know each other. Then trade contact information.

2. Be approachable – when others ask for your help, give them your attention, actively listen to understand them, be available. And be open-minded.

3. Be a questioner – good questions to get to know them, expresses interest in them, and finds their greatest skills and resources. And determines their needs.

4. Be a mentor – actively offer to be a guide, make useful suggestions, provide valuable resources to your connections. They will tend to do the same for you.

5. Be a connector-connector – seek out other connectors because the power of connectors being linked to other connectors is exponential. Vast resources.

In his 2002 book, *The Tipping Point,* author Malcom Gladwell notes: "their ability to span many different worlds is a function of something intrinsic to their personality, some combination of curiosity, self-confidence, sociability, and energy."

The bottom lines

Be a connector. Avoid being a networker business-card-collector. Build quality connections rather than quantities of connections. As a good connector, be friendly, approachable, questioning, a mentor, and connect with other connectors. Synergy.

Leadership Lesson 34

Your business is failing (and you don't know it)

Surprise! You have just discovered that your business, company, or corporation is failing. What took you so long? The red flags, warning buzzers, and sirens have been active for some time. Even when you were oblivious to them. Or ignoring them.

You might think that financial statements are your warning system. They are, but they are a lagging indicator. And sometimes too late. Question: what are some successful ways to spot trouble earlier? Answer: you can perform continuous self-examinations.

"Never underestimate your problem or your ability to deal with it." – Robert Schuller, clergy, author, speaker

Smoke signals ...

Turn on your business radar. Here are some critical warning signals to look for at all times (and suggested remedial actions to take) – long before your financial statements start flashing, "The end is near!"

Complacency – Loss of passion, attitude of "we've won" or "there is no competition," failure to maintain enthusiasm in the organization. Leaders must re-awaken the organization and themselves, instilling an energetic fresh sense of newness and excitement

Wrong People – Bad hiring practices, leaving some employees in the same job too long, retaining poor performers too long, not continuously training and upgrading people. Reassess the organization and replace weak spots with great new people. Train and upgrade the team, and visibly reward the best performers.

No standards – Not setting expectations, not constantly tracking actual results vs. plans, getting critical information too late, not periodically reviewing and updating standards and controls. Set standards and periodically review them. Communicate expectations and track actual performance against standards. Report results and celebrate goal achievements.

Poor customer service – Lack of respect, infrequent contact, failure to serve well, failure to ask customers how they are doing, failure to ask customers what they need now or need next, failure to up-sell customers. Demand that the sales and service teams follow a proven process to care deeply for customers. It costs far less to keep a customer than to find a new one.

Fire alarms ...

Mushy marketing – Failing to understand the market, poor planning and execution, lack of clear targets, unfavorable customer perception, poor positioning of products against competition and with customers. Obtain current market trends, update marketing programs and make certain that sales plans are aligned.

Stale Products – Not quickly staying with or ahead of market and customer needs, slow development processes, disconnects between products, production, processes, and marketing. Ensure constant teamwork among marketing, development and production. Get great new products to market, fast.

Stubbornness – Dogmatic adherence to the present and what has worked to date, failure to change quickly, failure to believe that constant change is mandatory. Always assess the entire business environment, internally and externally, and make fast changes - holding to the vision for the business.

Leaderless – The leader of a growing business has let go of the controls. There is a weakening of the essential things that created a good business: vision, mission, values, strategy and execution. It is time to regenerate the business, strengthen it and fly high again.

Paradox: we can only solve a problem once we know that we have one.

The bottom lines

No surprises. Find business problems continuously and solve them. Look into every part of the business: leadership, marketing, products, customer service, lack of standards and measurements, staffing. Don't ignore problems. Solve them.

Leadership Lesson 35

Getting results by harsh demands, effective expectations, and powerful intentions

Results. As a leader, how do you achieve good results? Several choices to weigh. Demand what you want. Expect good goals to be completed. Intend that great outcomes be realized. Which way to go?

Making hard demands might get a short-term result, but can create resentments, distrust, and angst. Setting expectations is a better choice for consistent effects – as long as expectations embrace reasonable outcomes. Powerful intentions can foster sometimes amazing results.

So, what is the best way to reach your goals – demands, expectations, intentions?

Harsh demands

In difficult business situations, leaders might need to demand an action to avoid a catastrophe. But if demands happen unnecessarily and too often, it is tantamount to crying, "Wolf, wolf!" Employees become anxious or disengaged.

Remember WorldCom? This telecom company of the 1990's grew rapidly into the second largest telecom player in the U.S. after AT&T. It evolved into MCI and then devolved into bankruptcy (later acquired by Verizon). CEO Bernie Ebbers, a demanding personality, was convicted of financial fraud and imprisoned for 25 years. Harsh demands can emerge from our "dark side."

"We were a fast-growing company, and I was a demanding boss." – Bernard Ebbers, former CEO of WorldCom

Effective expectations

Why set objectives without expectations that they be reasonably met? Teams can be motivated by good goals:
1. Build goals as a team, including those responsible for implementing them.
2. Clear, consistent communications is essential in creating good goals.
3. Don't waste time with impossible goals – they must be achievable.
4. Assign someone who is accountable overall for achieving the objective.
5. Set due dates for the completion of goals.
6. Establish a criterion for knowing when the full objective is met.
7. Track progress frequently – especially for critical goals.

Johnson Controls is a Fortune 500 company. Their Expectations Model for 170,000 employees "defines the expected behavior in support of our vision, values and goals."

Be careful about "hard expectations" of absolute outcomes. Rather, be flexible about the degree to which goals are met. Reasonable expectations arise from our intellect of experienced wisdom.

"I have no expectation of making a hit every time I come to bat." – Franklin D. Roosevelt, 32nd President of the United States

Powerful intentions

At a higher level, a number of universities, organizational developers, quantum physicists, and spiritual writers are researching and teaching the power of intention.

An excerpt from a 2013 *Harvard Business Review* article:

A 2007 book, "The Intention Experiment," explored the science of intention, drawing on the findings of leading scientists around the world. Author Lynne McTaggart uses cutting-edge research conducted at Princeton, MIT, Stanford, and other universities and laboratories to reveal that intent is capable of profoundly affecting all aspects of our lives.

The FedEx team intention is to move all packages to their destination safely, without damage, cost effectively, and within the time asked for by the customer. Powerful intention, powerful results. Creative intentions emanate from our inner being, our spirit, our soul.

"Our intention creates our reality." – Wayne Dyer, spiritual philosopher, author, teacher

The bottom lines

Results. Every leader wants them. How to achieve them? Demands are quick, but harsh. Expectations of achieving good goals is an intelligent norm. Intention setting from our innermost being is a newer method of allowing unexpected results to emerge. Stunning results.

Leadership Lesson 36

Be respected - 9 unbearable reasons why you are not

Oh, we all want it. Respect, that is. But all of us don't get it. Why not? Simple. We don't give it to others. Back to the Golden Rule: treat others as you would like to be treated. It works. One classic book sets this straight: *"How to Win Friends and Influence People"* by Dale Carnegie. Written decades ago, it is still among the top bestselling business books. Of all time.

But it is focused on the positive side of respect – and other positive human qualities. On the flip side, what are you doing to lose respect – and lose business? Read on.

"No one is going to stick their head out of the trenches for someone they don't respect or trust. You can get shot doing that." – Gordon Bethune, former CEO of Continental Airlines, board member of Honeywell, Sprint, Prudential

Losing respect

Here are 9 proven ways to lose respect in business (and in your personal life):

1. Lack of self-respect: if we do not have self-esteem and self-respect, then we cannot be truly respectful of others – and they will not respect us.

2. Fail to see and acknowledge the positive side of others: fault-finding, not thanking others for the good that they do, instilling fear, reprimanding people in front of others.

3. Not communicating openly and honestly: doing all the talking, failing to listen, having hidden agendas, not open to shared concerns and objectives.

4. Exhibiting negative behaviors: showing distain, discrimination of any kind, playing favorites with some members of the team, impatience, distrust, greed.

5. Character blemishes and outright defects: egotistical, no integrity, an array of dysfunctional behaviors, weak values.

6. Just plain bad manners: talking down to others, interrupting when others are speaking, showing no interest for the personal side of others, zero discretion.

7. Hard-hearted attitudes: strict adherence to the letter-of-the-law, no flexibility for the spirit-of-the-law, no tolerance for difference of opinions, stinginess, opinionated.

8. Negative attitudes: constant talk of failure, blaming others, expressed fear of competitors, not delegating due to distrust of others, complaining.

9. No authenticity: pretending to know things, dishonesty, claiming success for self and not giving credit to others, bragging, not vulnerable, unwilling to share personal life.

Whew! Quite a list. But even one of these things can rob a leader (and others) of respect by others. Time to change.

Gaining respect (a short list)

Genuinely be interested in other people. Smile a lot. Learn people's names and use them. Invite others to talk about themselves and honestly listen. Pay attention to the interests of others. Offer to help the other person. You are respecting them. And they will respect you.

How Big Blue does it

"Our basic belief is respect for the individual, for their rights and dignity. It follows from this principle that IBM should:
- Help each employee to develop their potential and make the best use of their abilities.
- Pay and promote on merit.
- Maintain two-way communications between manager and employee, with opportunity for a fair hearing and equitable settlement of disagreements."

The Bottom Lines

Respect. Mutual respect between people, including leaders, is the oil that lubricates successful businesses. Give up beliefs, attitudes, words, and behaviors that destroy respect. Including, lack of self-respect. Practice the Golden Rule. Genuinely be interested in other people. Be authentic. Be respected.

Leadership Lesson 37

Unambiguous disagreement and its creative power

Hate conflict? Too bad. Because there is always something to learn from clearly understood disagreement and honest difference of opinion. New ideas emerge, strong talent is identified, opportunities are uncovered. Sparks of success are ignited. But ...

It does not always work that way. Some are afraid to say what they believe. And others do not want to hear those who disagree with them. So why not build a culture where healthy disagreement is encouraged? The founder of a $5.3 billion food empire had it figured out. He knew that he could learn from open honest disagreement from others.

"In business, when two people always agree, one of them is irrelevant." William Wrigley, Jr., founder of the Wrigley Company, philanthropist

Shedding some sunlight

Sun Microsystems experienced significant disagreement with a good vendor during the planning phase for an important new product. Sun executives wisely asked for a meeting to clear the air. They did not want to waste a product opportunity nor lose a valued relationship with the vendor.

Both parties were invited to share their honest understandings, concerns, and assumptions. The lead Sun executive explained how he was thinking – and feeling – about the impact of a prior Sun management change on the situation. After a bit of silence, the vendor executive remarked that they felt the same way.

There was an instant relief, erroneous assumptions were erased, and a new agreement was reached that benefitted both parties. Out of disagreement was born a new opportunity for success for Sun.

Dissolving the great divide

Here are some effective ways to turn disagreement and disappointment into solutions and success:

Agree to disagree – don't hide it with your other "dead elephants under the table," admit that there is a conflict, and (if it is important) work to resolve it.

Confront now – don't wait until dissention becomes overheated and explodes, schedule a meeting right away to work on the issues.

Seek common ground – find out what both parties are looking for, find the similarities and differences, amplify the similarities to resolve the differences.

Just the facts – list the facts as each party sees them, again spot similarities, isolate and discuss the facts that differ, and why they differ.

Test for assumptions – are the facts really facts or are they assumptions, put assumptions aside for a while, and come back to examine them later.

Oh, that feeling – feelings matter so pay attention to them, ask the parties how they feel about the situation, knowing that exposure of feelings creates openness?

Isolate the risks – determine how significant the disagreement is, what impacts it has if unresolved, and the costs to the business.

List opportunities – ask the question, "If we resolve this, what new possibilities for products, markets, customers, and the business could we create?"

Surprise quiz – one of the most powerful questions to pose is, "What are we pretending not to know?" The answers will often lead to a winning resolution.

Check egos at the door. Resolving disputes involves respect for each other, eliminating personal attacks, and working in good faith for the organization – not personal gain.

The Bottom Lines

Disagree. It is not only OK, it can be creatively constructive. Build a culture that allows for healthy disagreement. Have a process for resolving valid dissention. Who knows, resolution of disagreements might create your next winning opportunity. And a better organization. Really!

Leadership Lesson 38

Stupefying courage as the guts of startup success

Get this. 90% of new business startups fail. That's according to *Forbes Magazine* January 2016. Why do they flop? Notably, 40% have no real market to begin with, per a recent *Fortune Magazine* article. Add bad products, poor startup team, lack of capital. And more.

Greater question: why do 10% succeed against the odds? Some say blind luck. Some would say insanity. Others might suggest that it is divine intervention. Perseverance, yes. Patience, of course. Powerful vision, uh huh. But the perspective of the winners is that undaunted courage is the sustaining stuff of success. Guts.

"And most important, have the courage to follow your heart and intuition." – Steve Jobs, founder of Apple, Inc.

Gorillas unstoppable

Apple, Inc. – Steve Jobs, Steve Wozniak, and Ronald Wayne founded Apple in 1976. Who knew it would become the world's largest tech company based on revenues and assets?

Steve and Woz knew. Ron did not. He sold his interest in 1977 for $800 and left. Today his missed-fortune would be worth over $70 billion. Woz left later with plenty of equity. But Steve Jobs had the courage to stay with his vision, even when it was blurred more than once. Courage.

Ford Motor Company – Henry Ford suffered through two prior automotive company startups. But his third attempt resulted in one of the world's greatest startup successes.

Henry not only had the grit to start over the third time, he gave us the gift of production assembly lines, overpaid happy employees, and the launch of an entire industry. Guts.

Amazon.com – Jeff Bezos founded this massive online retailer with three strikes against him: the distrust of people buying online; his own misperceived regret that he had waited too long to start the venture; and an unorthodox business plan that would not make money for five years.

Today Amazon is the largest retailer in the United States – larger than any store-based retailer including Walmart. Fearless.

Gnats undaunted

OK, not every great startup has the glamor of the gorillas. There are many that we would label as "ho-hum" businesses. Example:

Anita Roddick shopped at a Berkeley, California one-of-a-kind cosmetic store in 1970. They used natural ingredients, did not test on animals, and trained and employed immigrant women. In 1976 Anita started her own "The Body Shop," purchased the name from the Berkeley store, and started growing stores at 50% per year.

In 2006, she sold out to L'Oréal for $950 million. Today there are 2,600 stores worldwide. She was a courageous women's activist and philanthropist.

Creating courage

Courage is developed, not inborn. Here are some tips for building business boldness:

1. Accept uncertainty and keep moving forward.
2. Be "all in" and vulnerable to criticism.
3. Avoid trading your authenticity for approval.
4. Take risks and innovate in all areas of the business.
5. Establish tough goals, but strategic, measurable, achievable, realistic, and timely.

Think, speak, and act in courageous ways. Always.

The bottom lines

Starting a business? There is a 90% chance it will fail. Courage is the key quality for success. Whether you are creating an exotic technology corporation - or a mundane consumer goods company. Have the courage to continue against the odds. Guts.

Leadership Lesson 39

Loose dots, fuzzy connectors, and clear visions

Progress. You've come a long way and experienced business success. Yet you are not certain about how you got to this point. Some noticeable events have occurred along your path. Many people met and remembered. Events and people are your dots and connectors to be understood. Why?

Your professional thread. Once we understand the path of happenings and humans that formed and fostered our business lives, we can begin to see a picture of what lies ahead. An opportunity for more success.

"You can't connect the dots looking forward; you can only connect them looking backwards. So you have to trust that the dots will somehow connect in your future. You have to trust in something - your gut, destiny, life, karma, whatever. This approach has never let me down, and it has made all the difference in my life." – Steve Jobs, co-founder of Apple, Inc.

Unfolding the map

Looking at a roadmap after we have traveled gives us added and new perspectives of that journey. And often we are moved to look ahead at future travel. How to apply this principle in our professional journey? It is time to take a ride.

Spread out a large sheet of paper and, from the lower left to the upper right, start noting a year-by-year history of key events in your business career. Add the names of business associates, teachers, mentors, friends, and others who helped you. Enliven this journey by adding relevant pix, logos, business cards, and other memories.

OK, so we live in a digital world. Use your computer to create this atlas of achievements. Yes, failures are worth adding – we learned (hopefully) from them!

Your business biography

What is now in front of you is your autobiography of your professional migration at this point in your career. Here are seven learning questions to ask yourself:

1. What are the five most important events of my career and how are they connected?

2. Who are the five most influential people in my professional life and how to they relate to each other?

3. How are any of these people connected to some of the key events in my profession?

4. How did these events happen and how did I meet these people?

5. What was happening in my career just before these events occurred – and just prior to meeting these people?

6. What are the key themes and threads that pop out of my business biography?

7. What am I pretending not to know?

Now, spend some time in reflection and mediation and imagine what might be coming next in your professional path. Opportunity is at your door.

Magic memory

When a child, Joanne Rowling liked to write fantasy tales and read them to her little sister. Rowling lived in poverty until she wrote a book for youth about wizardry. "Harry Potter and the Philosopher's Stone" appeared in1997. Today, J.K. Rowling is renowned for her "Harry Potter" book series of over 400 million copies sold.

The bottom lines

What's next for you? Determine the important events and people who most influenced your career. These are the dots and connectors that can frame your future. Visually diagram this pathway and self-analyze it. Your next career step is emerging from the field of all possibilities. Opportunity knocks. Again.

Leadership Lesson 40

Repairing the ruins of strong skills and bad behaviors

Cognitive. The contemporary buzzword that universities use to describe how we learn to do things. Including job skills. We acquire that knowledge and understanding via cognition – learning through our thoughts, experiences, and senses. Knowing how to do something. Cognitive skills.

Here's the problem. If our behaviors (our "soft skills") do not support our good work skills, the practical application of our talent is largely wasted. Example: how can we effectively delegate when we are poor communicators, not trusted, and uncaring? Can't.

People are hired for their skills and fired for their behaviors. – Anon

Remember Enron?

"The Smartest Guys in the Room" was the stunning documentary movie that portrayed a brilliant corporate staff that rocketed Enron Corporation to amazing heights of success. For a while. Formed in 1985 by merging two smaller companies, this energy giant employed 20,000 people and had stated revenues of $100 billion by year 2000. It was named "America's Most Innovative Company" by *Fortune Magazine* for six consecutive years.

But the collectively smart folks that ignited the company success also embraced a collectively bad behavior. They lied. Enron died of rapid bankruptcy brought on by a systemic, systematic reporting of fraudulent financial information. Dead by year 2004.

The entire company lost their jobs. Several of the smartest guys went to prison. A skillful success. A behavioral disaster.

The Do's and the Be's

Skills and behaviors. How to do things, and how to be while doing them. Business media gives us lists of the most important cognitive skills of great leaders. But not so much about the behaviors – especially behaviors that make effective use of good skills.

Here are key skills exhibited by successful leaders – and critical behaviors that support these skills:

Skill: Setting the Vision
Behaviors: strategic thinking, visionary view, steadfast belief

Skill: Empowering People
Behaviors: trusting relationships, honest communications, forgiving attitude

Skill: Effective Communications
Behaviors: authentic talk, open conversations, active listening

Skill: Developing Culture
Behaviors: environmentally aware, honesty for all, affirmative attitude

Skill: Organizing Work
Behaviors: seeing details, bias to action, priority focused

More ...

Skill: Solving Problems
Behaviors: supportive concern, intentional resolution, resourceful attention

Skill: Driving to Results
Behaviors: a bias to action, inspiring communications, affirmative outlook

Skill: Creating Innovation
Behaviors: promoting new ideas, strategic viewpoint, allowing failure

Skill: Focusing Priorities
Behaviors: interactive communications, organizational view, envisioning results

Strong leadership skills with accompanying supportive behaviors multiplies an organizations opportunity for accelerated growth and sustainable success. Period.

"Return on Behavior"

The operating skills of good leaders are judged by financial measures: Return on Investment, Return on Sales, Return on Equity, etc. But an April 2015 *Harvard Business Review* article titled "Return on Character" was based upon the key behaviors, the character, of their executives. Using the financial measure of return on assets (ROA), the high-character companies produced an exceptionally high ROA of 9.35% and the low-character organizations provided a miserably low 1.93% ROA. Proof.

The bottom lines

Leadership skills. There are many lists of what successful business leaders know how to do. Leadership behaviors. There are fewer lists of the key behaviors that strong leaders know how to be. The best leaders have both. Knowing how to get things done – and knowing how to behave while doing them. Capabilities and character. Success.

Leadership Lesson 41

Here are 5 ways to be an Early Adapter (not Early Adopter)

Oh, yes. For years we have learned about being an "Early Adopter." The gotta-have-it-first technoids who sleep in front of the Apple Store to buy the first new iThing. At any cost. Likewise, some businesses want emerging technologies in order to create advanced systems. These buyers are the early adopters of products. First in line.

Wait. The "Early Adapter." This is another type of early bird for something new. But it is not about technology and products. It is about new ways of doing things. New business processes, streamlined planning, faster innovation techniques. New competition, new geographies, new everything. The early adapters are first to benefit.

"Adapt or perish, now as ever, is nature's inexorable imperative." – H. G. Wells, scientist, writer, historian, teacher

Adios business plan, ciao business model

Decades of five-year business plans that took a year to prepare, filled three three-ring binders that nobody read, and were out of date before they were finished.

Change. The newer business model subsumed the old business plan. The model succinctly describes the business process, including purpose, target customers, offerings, organizational structures, sourcing, trading practices, operational methods, policies, culture, everything. Capturing maximum value. The guts of a business plan. On one page!

The Early Adapters of the Business Model were – guess who? Entrepreneurs who were drawn to the idea of capturing value from a simple depiction of all the moving parts of a business. And the ease of pivoting the model when necessary or desirable. Anytime.

The Flexibles

Who are they? They are the Early Adapters. A family of business people who understand the need to adapt to change. Often quickly. They are trend-spotters with accurate built-in radars and they know what is going on around them. Quick to see new ways of thinking and doing things.

Here are five keys to being a flexible, Early Adapter:

Reality check – understand the truth about the external and internal influences on your business and look for potentially impactful changes. Sooner, not later. This provides an early edge to dealing with transitions and transformations, calamity and confusion.

Think system – not situation. When seeing a possible (or likely) need for change, consider the impact on the entire business, a business unit or division. Not just headquarters. What about remote offices and factories?

Weakest spot – where is the Achilles Heel in the business? What innovations in terms of new processes, new ways of doing business, streamlined methods, cutting areas of bloat, will help? Forget radical new technology. Until it is not so radical anymore.

Ask others – if you think you know where rapid adaptation is needed, you are missing an opportunity. Ask your organization. Collectively they know more than you and your immediate reports do. Assume nothing. Get the facts. Then adapt.

Adaptive investment – the University of Pennsylvania researched 3,000 companies and found that investing 10% of revenue for capital improvements increased productivity by 4%. The same investment in people boosted productivity over 8%.

Be an Early Adapter of innovative, effective business methods – not just more cool technology.

The Bottom Lines

Change accelerates. Leaders tend to be Early Adopters of cool technologies to manage change. An alternative is to be an Early Adapter of innovative business methods to leverage change. And consider a blend of Adaption and Adoption to surf the infinite waves of change. For better business.

Leadership Lesson 42

Ditch mediocrity and join "The Accountables"

Disconnect. Big one. Being accountable is a prized behavior of leaders, managers, and individuals. Accountability is in the infinite lists of Top Ten characteristics for successful business people. From CEO's to all co-workers. Understandable when looking at getting things done and reaching goals. But.

34% of leaders do not hold others accountable for results – per 2014 research by the Brandon Hall Group. The damage done by not being accountable, and not expecting others to be accountable, is enormous. Many leaders and others are not aware of the famous plaque on a U.S. president's White House desk. He was accountable.

The Buck Stops Here. – Harry S. Truman, 33rd President of the United States

"The Accountables"

Who are they? These are the business people and others who are personally willing to answer for their decisions, actions, and outcomes. They do not blame others for their failures, they are quick to fix things, and they strive to make things better.

Accountable leaders and others ask good questions and find the best answers. They are champions of opportunities for success – the success of their companies and organizations.

Responsibility is different than accountability, but they are related. Your responsibility is your job, duty, task, or function. It is a role for which you are in charge. Being accountable for and within your responsibility will help you succeed. And vice-versa.

Bad news, good news

When leaders and others are not accountable, or expect others to be answerable, here are some of the negative impacts on the organization:

- Teams not developed – a team without accountability is not a team (really).
- Employees not coached – an accountable leader will mentor and train their people.
- Communications not clear – sloppy communications will foster poor results.
- Culture of mediocrity – when leaders do not expect accountability, they won't get it.
- Goals not met – watch performance, profitability, and pride go to the wasteland.

But when accountability by all, and for all, is woven into the culture of the organization, this is what happens:

- Trusting within and among teams – mutual respect grows, teams strengthen.
- Supporting responsibility – responsibility without accountability is a zero.
- Infusing the culture – accountable people are winners and others will follow.
- Attaining goals – in order to meet performance goals, we must be accountable.
- Amplifying momentum – "We're on a roll!" becomes the norm.

Accountability is a central pillar of effective organizational development and success.

"Unto thine own self be true"

Self-accountability? It is normal to feel and act accountable to one's manager – our jobs generally depend upon it. But, how accountable are we when "no one is watching."

The self-accountable person begins with an inner desire to be accountable as a key component in their way of life – both personally and professionlly. And in Abraham Maslow's model of human needs, an internal propellant to ascend his pyramid into slef motivation and self-actualization.

When you have a well-developed sense of self-accountability, you are honest with yourself, and are answerable and responsible for what you say and do. You have personal ethics. – Massage Today Magazine

The bottom lines

Be accountable. Expect accountability. Even though one-third of U.S. business leaders do not. The price of poor accountability is very high. The benefits of accountable leaders and teams is even higher. Begin with your own accountability. Self-accountability.

Leadership Lesson 43

Stop stalling and get your action in gear

Growing pressure. From within. The nagging notion that there is something more for you to do. Constant creation is the way of the universe and it calls us to move (and move again). Providing products and services of value. Feeling free.

Resistance. Another internal pressure – to stand still and do nothing. Why? Fear: we might fail, it's too much work, or it doesn't matter. Worse, fear of success. We are bloated with opportunities, but blocking ourselves from creating good. Feeling frozen.

"Nothing happens until something moves." – Albert Einstein, Nobel Prize winning physicist, philosopher

Fear and excitement

What an uncanny mix. Fear and excitement are both felt when we are heading into a new creative endeavor. Not just art. Anything. New job, new career, new processes, products, services. New businesses, organizations, and people.

We are born to create and we feel frustrated when we are not being innovative. Classic case: "I am going to write a book – it has been on my mind for years." Excitement of seeing the book published. Fear of the time and effort in writing it. Excitement-fact: estimates of U.S. people who want to write a book range from 80% to 90%. Fear-fact: only 3% of Americans actually write and publish "the book." Even fewer start one.

What's missing? Action. Simply taking the first step and keep moving. What's not missing? Procrastination.

Procrastination fascination

Not starting something creative and important that we want to do is a paradox. So why do we procrastinate? *Psychology Today* June 17, 2016, offers some reasons and remedies:

1. No structure – we favor impulse over decision. It is easier to check Facebook than to it is to start moving on something creative. Stay off the playgrounds of the Internet and other distractions. Purposeful creative activity takes work and gives meaning.

2. "Unpleasant" task – we convince ourselves that an innovative endeavor is too big, difficult, and time consuming. Just break it down into bite-sized daily chunks. Start with the first chunk today. Do more every day for a minimum number of hours.

3. Time gap – we fail to connect short-term efforts with long-term rewards. So we delay again. E.g., an immediate discomfort of jumping into a cold pool masks the future benefits of swimming laps. Instead, connect the plunge to the energy of exercise.

4. Awful anxiety – we use avoidance to dance around it. We avoid starting. Paradox: we avoid the stress of starting and create even more stress by more procrastination. Focus on the rewards and imagine the project completed. Feel success.

5. Low self-confidence – we develop doubts about our abilities. We miss opportunities to gain new knowledge and skills. But goal-attainment tends to raise our feelings of self-confidence. And this can cause us to take on even more challenging goals.

Encores. Here are successful people who went on to do even more: Thomas Edison, Steve Jobs, Steven Spielberg. Serial innovators for good. Doing good for others and feeling good about it. Starters, not procrastinators.

The bottom lines

No stalling. Don't suffer by inaction. You have an inner urge to give to others – first time and more times. What's the problem? Procrastination, which is uncomfortable self-sabotage. Take the first step to fulfillment. Dump delays and distractions. Get off your greatest asset and move. Act.

Leadership Lesson 44

Swing from loss to profit in 5 easy steps of follow-through

Golf swing. Most duffers forget a critical component of a good golf swing. The ending. Follow-through. Too focused on hitting the ball vs. developing a great swing. Follow-through swings win golf games. Follow-up action wins business. Why?

Follow up is key to finishing. We have and wonderful ways to put them into action – when, as leaders, we invoke responsibility, delegation, action, and accountability. All good things. Unless they are not brought to closure and completion. Going nowhere.

Remember: 34% of leaders do not hold others accountable. Why? No follow-up.

So, what's wrong?

No consistent process for follow-up. Sure, in software development it is popular to have morning standup meetings to rate progress and resolve problems. And, every successful salesperson relentlessly follows through with all their leads, prospects, and customers. However.

Other business functions can be follow-through weaklings. Projects in marketing, engineering, administration, accounting, production can lag. Nobody in charge of follow-up. Costly.

A recent report from the Project Management Institute notes that, "Due to poor project performance, global organizations waste an average of $122 million for every $1 billion spent on projects."

Call the psychologist

What causes poor follow-up? Here are some irrational excuses:

- Takes too much time – we need to apply our energy to the project.
- Nobody cares – management is not asking us how we are doing.
- It is difficult – asking teams for updates and holding meetings is cumbersome.
- It won't matter – the project will move ahead at its own pace anyway.
- We have not needed it in the past – we got things done without follow-up.
- The team members should do it – somebody else should not have to babysit.

As a leader, do not buy any of these reasons. Put follow-up processes in place – and then follow-up on the processes. Be accountable and hold others accountable.

Five easy steps

Here are five proven ways to establish and maintain good follow-through practices in your organization:

1. Make projects and activities visible – the more important, the more visible. Consider using a team-based software tool to track all projects and report them. Consistently.

2. Appoint follow-up leaders – someone responsible for timely tracking to make certain that everything about a project is recorded, up to date and reported. Clearly.

3. Centralize communications – team members and others provide status inputs to the follow-up leader. And that person informs everyone about their project. Constantly.

4. Solve issues quickly – no hiding from challenges and no punishment for having them. Instead, promote fast failures and faster recovery from them. Courageously.

5. Reward progress – provide verbal, written, and gift recognitions to the follow-through leaders and their teams who achieve on-time delivery of their projects. Celebratory.

Note that Apple assigns a DRI (directly responsible individual) who is accountable for every task. Zero confusion about who is tagged to move the action forward.

Mary Kay knew

"Those who are blessed with the most talent don't necessarily outperform everyone else. It's the people with follow-through who excel." – Mary Kay Ash, American business woman, founder of $3.5 billion cosmetics company, Mary Kay, Inc.

The bottom lines

Don't wait. Even before a critical project or single action has started, assign someone to follow-up. Or do it yourself. Or both. Remember, 34% of leaders do not enforce accountability for actions. Too easy to let things slide. Including an entire business.

Leadership Lesson 45

Purge old stuff and make room for more profit

Let go. Get rid of unneeded stuff. Inventory and things of no value. Infrastructure and organization that is not productive. Ideas, beliefs and attitudes that are worn out. Things that only take up space – physical and mental.

Why? Make room for something better. Fresh inventory and processes, productive reorganization and new hires, new ideas and plans that will accelerate growth. What's the blockage? Lethargy. It is easier to coast than to cut.

When you remove layers, simplicity and speed happen. – Ginni Rometty, Chair, President, and CEO of IBM

Bloated inventory

Free money. Per a *Forbes* article example, reduce production inventory from a four-week supply to three weeks and annual savings would be 67% of the one-week cost reduction. Spell that "big savings."

Obsolete or idle inventory? Get rid of everything you can. Sell it off, give it away (take a tax break if possible), clean up your balance sheet, save space.

Lottsa old stuff in storage? Dump it. If it is in your own facility, use the space for something productive. If it is off site, consider this: the cost of self-storage grows faster than inflation each year. And, at least 15% of those surveyed by *New York Times Magazine* noted that the content of their storage was unneeded. More free money.

Fat infrastructure

What is your organizational productivity? E.g., how many dollars of operating profit do each of your FTE (full time equivalent employees, including consultants and temps) generate?

What has this number been for each of the past five years? Is the trend up or down? Do you have too many FTE's? If so, why? This can eat your profits and your organization alive. The largest expense in companies is labor – 60% of total expenses. And growing.

Or, reorganize and place underutilized people in areas that need help. Increase productivity and energize the organization. Beats layoffs.

Overweight ideas

Amazing. Some very large corporations, and small businesses, hang onto old ways of thinking, speaking, and acting. The original American Airlines nosedived when they failed to watch the takeoff of upstart startups such as Southwest.

Kodak shot their film-based business into a dark place while Canon, Nikon, and others focused on the digital photo opportunity. And, the smart folks who created smart phones also shot the panoramic view of life captured and transmitted anytime, anywhere. Ask Apple.

And we hang onto old worn out beliefs, ideas, and situations. Even when they are not working out. Or worse, destructive. Time to let them go and replace them with fresh, new, exciting thoughts, words and actions. Ideas that build and rebuild great businesses. From Amazon to Zale.

The Purge Team

Interesting. We spend most of our time dreaming up the new (or want to, but don't). But how much energy do we expend taking a look at the old stuff? Too little. Form a small cross-function team to search out and remove the old, wasteful, unnecessary blockages to streamlined success.

The Bottom Lines

Start purging and get rid of old stuff that has rotted and moved from useful to useless. Robbing your bottom line. Dump inventory and storage. Reduce or reorganize (or both) unnecessary infrastructure. Flush boring old ideas and attitudes – replace them with creative fresh dreams. Go new, grow profits.

Leadership Lesson 46

See how failure is another word for success

Lists. Oh, you've read them. The ongoing lists of reasons businesses fail. Insufficient capital, no market, poor product, weak staffing, fuzzy vision. But how much have you learned about the value of failure? Likely little. It seems too much like reading an obituary. Downer.

Yet there is value in failure – if we can see it. Something to learn, things not to repeat, different ways to do things, new perceptions about ourselves and others. We can see failure as final. The end of a hard journey. Or we can see failure as a worthwhile detour to a faster road of success. Our choice.

Success if not final, failure is not fatal: it is the courage to continue that counts. – Winston Churchill, British statesman

The beholding eye

What is failure, anyway? Here are five variations of so-called "failure":

1. Bankruptcy – yet some companies reorganize, emerge stronger, and more than pay off debts. General Motors declared bankruptcy in 2008, was rescued by federal loans, got rolling again, and repaid all loans plus a profit to our government.

2. Ending – a Kansas City cartoonist failed with an early Laugh-O-Gram film enterprise. He took a train to Los Angeles while Imagineering his business, and re-opened under Walt Disney & Company. Eventual net worth = $1.1 billion.

3. Exiting – the business is successfully merged into, or sold to, another business. At one point, Sun was among the top tech companies in the world with 35,000 employees. After sustaining losses, it was sold to Oracle Corporation for $7.4 billion.

4. Pivot – a startup, Odeo, entered the podcast network business. But Apple podcasts stopped Odeo, who was then approached by a student with a unique text messenger. Odeo rebirthed the company as Twitter. A historical pivot.

5. Combo – a troubled company with a good team purchases (or merges in) another troubled company with good products and brand. USAir acquired American Airlines, kept American's name, and is now the world's largest airline by revenues and profits.

Like beauty, failure is in the eye of the beholder. Almost invariably, business failures generate additional opportunity, resistance to repeat failures, and more innovation within (and among) industries.

The Resilients

Individuals "fail" as well – just like companies. Those who bounce back are historically amazing. E.g.:

Henry Ford declared bankruptcy in 1903. After more failures, he saw the reality of his dream emerge in the Ford Motor Company. His estimated net worth today would be $188 billion. And, his products serve millions of people globally. Failure?

Milton Hershey bankrupted himself after a failed candy store of six years. He created another company, perfected caramel production, and sold it for $1 million. Then he created The Hershey Company and perfected milk chocolate production. Want some?

Abraham Lincoln went bankrupt in 1833 when his general store failed. He eventually lost everything and worked for years to repay his debts. Elected as the 16th U.S. President in 1860, he is consistently known as our greatest president. Role model?

Endless examples point out that most successful people have had one or more failures that would stop most. But not the courageous.

The Bottom Lines

Redefine "failure." To fail and get up for another try is the mark of success. Those who persist most often reach their goals. Clue: learn from failure rather than either repeating the same mistakes. Or just quitting. Ever.

Leadership Lesson 47

Big cracks in your company vision and how to repair them

Get set, go! The organization's vision has been established and communicated by the leadership. A good team is on board. Action plans are delegated. What can go wrong? Everything.

Hold it – it is a big, bold vision. Start a new industry, provide unheard of new products and services, slay competitors. Conquer the world. What's the matter?

Myth: a vision is the guarantee for automatic business success in large corporations and small businesses. Truth: a vision must be clear, creative, compelling, concise, communicated. Unique and futuristic as well. And doable. Or nobody will buy into it – employees nor customers. No sale.

What is vision, really?

There is often confusion among mixed terms: vision, mission, values, strategy. Here are some clarifying descriptions:

Vision – what will the company look like in the future?
Example – our customer's data is never hacked.

Mission - what is the nature of the business, who does it serve, what does it provide?

Example - we provide small-medium businesses with high-value, tailored computer networks.

Values – what are the company's essential beliefs, attitudes, and behaviors?
Example – we earn trust, are obsessed with accuracy, and are committed communicators.

Strategy – what is the overall direction of the company to best utilize our resources?
Example - Offer additional integrated value-added products to existing and new customers.

Note that vision casts a forward view and forms a focal point of activity for employees, vendors, and others. And it can be a compelling attractor for customers.

Smoky pipe dreams

Yes, there are smudgy visions, too. Here are some that don't light up the imagination; they:

1. Lack a winning idea that differentiates the company from its competitors.
2. Tend to be mushy, trite, and hard to understand and communicate.
3. Are so improbable that people will not enroll in them.
4. Confuse mission statements with vision descriptions.
5. Do not look forward.

The only thing worse than having no sight is having no vision. – Helen Keller, blind author and lecturer

Winning visions

Look how big, compelling visions can turn dreams into reality:

Amazon – "Our vision is to be earth's most customer-centric company; to build a place where people can come to find and discover anything they might want to buy online." Now King-Konging the entire retail industry – including grocers.

Disney – "To make people happy." They obviously are: world's second largest media company; $55 billion revenue; 200,000 employees; worldwide presence; family favorite.

Facebook - "People use Facebook to stay connected with friends and family, to discover what's going on in the world, and to share and express what matters to them." 25% of the world's population is on Facebook.

Google – "To organize the world's information and make it universally accessible and useful." Revenues $90 billion in less than 20 years; global penetration; Google it.

Uber – ""make transportation as reliable as running water, everywhere, for everyone." From 0 to 60 billion $ in 8 years. And running the traditional taxi business into the ditch.

"Leadership is the capacity to translate vision into reality." – Warren Bennis, author, educator, and pioneer in leadership studies

The bottom lines

Get a vision. Not just any vision. Hold a vision that is compelling, understood, looks to the future – and is doable. A vision that your team and your customers will buy into. A vision that pulls the company to sustainable success. From dream to reality. Really.

Leadership Lesson 48

When business drama ends, leadership maturity begins

Oh, oh. Our leader is acting out again. Visibly and audibly irritated, blaming someone, and thrashing for immediate solutions. Without knowing what the problem really is – or even if there is a true problem. Drama.

It gets worse. Demeaning someone or an entire team. Name calling, threatening to fire people, and generally lashing out. Claiming legal action without basis. Referring to competitors and calling them better. Stomachs are tightened and the silence is a siren.

Not a shred of dignity. Not a leader. Really.

Bad act

Can't happen to you? Get dramatic, push too far, blast people inside and outside the organization, talk down to employees and others, and push the rules over the line.

Uber, the high-riding startup that grabbed the independent driver market, is troubled. Why? Founder/CEO, Travis Kalanick, became hyper-abrasive and vocalized it. Ran over the curb of civility. His board terminated him when Uber hit the wall of public disgust. Earlier Kalanick quote: "I'm like fire and brimstone sometimes."

Crash damage? Uber's main competitor, Lyft, has now raised $600 million for the race. Their U.S. market share climbed from 21.2% to 24.7% in just four months – while Uber's ride-share has stalled from 90% to 75% in two years. Next lap.

Exit stage left

Here are the *Ten Laws of Anti-Drama in the Workplace:*

1. First, don't bring your drama to meetings. Be certain you are not needing some attention. Your problem solvers will want to leave instead. Stop the drama.

2. Negative employees might need drama to feed their bad attitude. And it can be a deflection when they have nothing to contribute. Deal with repeat offenders.

3. Drama is an option, a choice. If we catch ourselves and others headed into drama, we can stop and get back to problem solving. We are stronger than our drama.

4. Do not waste energy. Drama depletes it. Good energy can be applied to describing the challenge at hand. And then finding creative team-based solutions.

5. Is there really a problem? Seriously, some people will describe a problem that is not a problem just to be noticed or a "hero." Describe issues thoroughly.

6. Let people know when they act out in drama. They might not know it. Tell them in private, and describe the negative effects. Terminate the persisting Drama Queens.

7. Calm counts. When leaders are calm, others will tend to be. If riled, settle down and then get down to solving problems. Don't be sponged up into others' drama.

8. Listen more than you talk. Get through the weeds and run around the ends of drama. Listening will help you bypass drama and focus instead on the challenges.

9. Maybe it isn't drama. Someone might simply want us to just listen. Stop trying to figure anything out – and be present for them (but don't keep repeating it with them).

10. We can learn from drama. About ourselves, others, and how to better handle drama. And, we can learn more about effective problem solving.

Difficulty is inevitable; drama is a choice. – Anita Renfroe, American Comedian

The bottom lines

Kill drama. It is a choice to make. Drama saps energy, de-focuses us and our teams, and is an obstacle to efficient problem solving. Learn the *Ten Laws of Anti-Drama in the Workplace*. Exit Drama Queens stage left. Encore.

Leadership Lesson 49

Short circuit negative energy - free yourself of complaints

Gloom. Doom. But the sky isn't falling – yet. Sagging, maybe. Outside the workplace, we talk about negative energies, how they are generated, how we feel them, and their minus impact on our lives. What about within our careers, jobs, and work? Zap!

Worst case? A chronic complaining leader (hint: they are not a real leader). Their negative energy penetrates an entire organization. People working in fear, subterranean communications, declining productivity. Escalating employee turnover costs. Bad reputation. Rotting elephants under the table. Smell of death.

"Complaining isn't a strategy." – Jeff Bezos, founder, chair, CEO of Amazon

Where complaints roll

Judgment. We compare an existing situation to what we think it should be. We fail to get actual facts, go emotional, and start griping. The Complain Game is started, followed by the Blame Game. Rather than defining the real problem, we blame someone. An executive, an employee, a vendor. Even a customer.

Case: The Firestone Tire and Ford Motor relationship went flat after 100 years. Certain tires sold to Ford were failing. Firestone leadership complained that Ford had high rollover rates on Explorer SUVs, blaming Ford for the problem. But the rollover rate was no higher on the Explorer than with competitive SUV's. Also, Explorer rollovers were less frequent with Goodyear Tires. Ford had the facts.

While Ford leadership voluntarily spent $3 billion to recall tires, Firestone was forced to recall 15 million tires – and pay $250M in damages to Ford. Ford cancelled the relationship of 100 years. Firestone lost a major customer. Complain, blame, and lose.

How to kill complaints

It is easier to complain than to take action to resolve the problem. Some will complain just to be noticed, look important, or avoid work. And, it is easy to make up things to complain about. Sometimes, complaining is just a version of gossip. Here are ways to contain complainers:

1. If a leader, do not be a complainer yourself. It is a sign of weakness, it spreads into your team, dampens productivity, and hurts the reputation of the organization.

2. As a leader, you can teach your organization to convert complaining into taking positive action to resolve issues. Using their energy to get facts and solve problems.

3. Remove chronic complainers from your team. They are toxic and will tend to bring down others – and breed other complainers. Even one can contaminate the team.

4. Individuals, avoid being a complainer. You will develop a negative reputation, negatively impact others, and may limit future opportunities. Including your job.

5. When you feel like complaining about someone else, consider getting to know them. You might find that they are facing challenges in their work and lives.

Obviously discern when someone provides valid input, such as a dangerous weakness in a facility vs. someone who does not like the company logo.

Complaint-Free Week

Try this. Stop complaining for one week in your workplace. If you fail during the week, start over. You will eventually train yourself to stop griping. Invite your team to play. No complaints allowed.

The bottom lines

Stop complaining. Really. It is a bad habit, debilitating to the complainer and those around them. Leaders who complain are ineffective pseudo-leaders. Individual complainers are toxic and not respected. Learn how to stop complaining and start solving problems. Try a Complaint-Free Week. Smile.

Leadership Lesson 50

Assassinate confusion with five bullet questions

Disorder. Lack of clarity immobilizes people, organizations, and entire companies. When the key drivers of a business are unclear, doubt, ignorance, and instability spread. Momentum slows. And a state of suspended animation appears. Worry.

The core issue is confusion. About one or more critical components of your business plan: purpose, vision, mission, values, culture, organizational structure, leadership and management, goals and objectives, strategy, priorities, actions. The antidote to confusion is clarity. And the answers to important questions create clarity. Just ask.

Find out fast where the confusion lies. To wait is to worsen the foggy lens of understanding.

Mud race

Start asking your organization for their inputs about what is not clear – and problems that are being caused as a result. Build a list of unclear areas and assign key leaders and managers to dig out the important facts associated with those areas. Soon.

Create special teams to address the unknowns. Prioritize the list and start at the top. Consider both the long-term issues (e.g., the Purpose and Vision are hazy) and short-term (e.g., key Actions are not well stated nor delegated. Both are important – and everything in between. Your business plan could have fatal fractures.

Confusion is the main cause of worry. – Dale Carnegie, American writer, corporate trainer

Just. Get. Clarity.

The power is in the question. So start asking these five questions about each of the top areas of cloudy confusion:

What?
- Define the area of confusion; what part of the business plan is being affected?
- What are the key negative impacts on the organization?
- Can you relate the probable and possible causes of the issue?

Why?
- Is there a reason why this concern has come to the surface now?
- Why wasn't this issue raised before now? Was it lurking beneath the surface?
- Is there more than one contributing reason for this problem?

When?
- How long has this dilemma existed; when was it first recognized?
- What is the timeframe when this situation can be resolved?
- When can we have a plan to fix the problem, including periodic progress reports?

Where?
- Are there specific parts of the organization that are particularly affected?
- Is the problem known outside of the company, and where?
- Where can we find resources around the company to get this dealt with, quickly?

Who?
- Who are the people in the organization who can best resolve this problem?

- Team leaders are important; who are they?
- Who else needs to know about this?

Here is a bonus question: how can we best communicate the situation in an open, honest, timely manner – and to whom?

From chaos to clarity

Organizations thrive when they are clear about what needs to get done, who needs to do it, and how it should get done. With clarity, everyone can pull together for a common cause. Without clarity, there is wasted effort and even chaos. In his analysis of Ewing Kauffman's company, Marion Laboratories, Gerald W. Holder attributed the organization success to an entrepreneurial leadership team that focused significant energy on creating clarity throughout the work force. – Kauffman Foundation, entrepreneurship.org

The Bottom Lines

Clarity. Constantly. The chaos of confusion is costly – and unnecessary. Ask great questions, get great answers, and build a great organization. What, why, when, where, who? These are the important bulleted questions to ask. Kill confusion. Worry less. Sleep better.

Leadership Lesson 51

Employee disengagement vs. best companies to work for

No secret. Every year one or more media members release their lists of the best companies to work for. No surprise. The very top ones are repeat performances: Google, KPMG, SAS, Salesforce, Whole Foods, Southwest Airlines. And some you might not be aware of. Kimley-Horn, Burns & McDonnell, Workday. How do some companies make it into these lists?

Example: *Fortune* works annually with *Great Places to Work* to uncover the cultures of organizations for inclusion in the annual *Fortune list of 100 Best Companies to Work For*. Special surveys are sent to employees of companies to obtain a score. Other means, such as *Glassdoor*, assess work environments through the eyes of employees.

What really matters? You might expect some answers and you'd be right. But there are some surprise factors, too. Read on.

What's different?

Remember that over 50% of the U.S. workforce is not engaged. And has not been for a long time. But what fosters employee engagement in the best companies? Here are some key factors found in random surveys of employees:

- Trust – the level of trust between employees and management is a critical factor. This relationship is foundational to other key measurements. And mutual respect, credibility, and fairness are key underlying supports for strong trust.

- Pride – employees have a relationship with their work and, when favorable, they take pride in their job, organization, and company. They feel purposeful and fulfilled – and they are inclined to be engaged – and stay engaged.

- Fraternity – an overall feeling of being part of something bigger than one's self – yet at the same time individuals are valued. The culture is open, friendly, and inviting, with a community feeling throughout.

The higher the ratings in these areas, the better the company is to work for. In fact, in The *Great Places to Work* "Trust Index" survey, 67% of a company score is based upon the above factors. Important.

There's more …

Culture is critical. Again, employees in high scoring companies were asked about compensation, benefits, communications, recognition and rewards, diversity, hiring methods.

One business reporter found that employees in best companies to work for are drawn by an opportunity to be part of giving back. Most of the companies in these lists have company philanthropy programs that connect employees to their communities and the world. It matters.

Purpose-driven. This is an increasing conversation because people want work to be an experience that is meaningful. Why does this matter? Gallup's polling answer:
- 32% of employees are engaged
- 51% are not engaged
- 17% are actively disengaged and creating trouble

Who's on top for 2017?

Here are the top ten of *Forbes 100 Best Companies to Work 2017:* Google, Wegmans Food Markets, The Boston Consulting Group, Baird, Edward Jones, Genentech, Ultimate Software, Salesforce, Acuity, Quicken Loans.

And 12 companies have make the list every year for 20 consecutive years, including Publix, REI, and Goldman Sachs.

By putting the employee first, the customer effectively comes first by default, and in the end, the shareholder comes first by default as well. – Richard Branson, English businessman, philanthropist

The bottom lines

Stop employee disengagement. It is costly. Instead be a best place to work. Use mutual respect, credibility, and fairness to build strong trust. Foster employee pride and camaraderie. Create a welcoming culture. Support philanthropy. Be a best company.

Leadership Lesson 52

Too busy playing manager to be an effective leader?

Misfire. You are supposed to be the leader of the company. Or of an organization or project. Creating vision and bringing the team along with you. But it is not working out. Instead you are spending most of your time organizing and getting things done. Managing, not leading.

Aren't they the same – leading and managing? Not really. Some similarities, and many differences. Both are concerned about creating success.

Management is efficiency in climbing the ladder of success; leadership determines whether the ladder is leaning against the right wall. Stephen R. Covey, educator, author, businessman

What's the difference?

Here are ten ways to understand the overall characteristics of both managers and leaders.

1. Leaders create and communicate the vision; managers follow the vision.
2. Leaders lead people; managers manage processes.
3. Leaders take the first step; managers take the next step.
4. Leaders ask "why" and "what;" managers ask "how" and "when."
5. Leaders align people; managers organize people.
6. Leaders motivate and inspire; managers administrate and control.

7. Leaders mentor, teach, and pull; managers coach, tell, and push.
8. Leaders challenge the status quo; managers work with the status quo.
9. Leaders unleash potential; managers coordinate resources.
10. Leaders build organizations; managers assemble teams.

So, if you are supposed to be the leader, but find yourself drowning in managerial activities, you are obstructing yourself from being a good leader. Somebody needs to change. Guess who?

Note ...

There is often overlap between the roles of leaders and managers. Many great leaders also are excellent managers. And many strong managers can learn to become effective leaders.

It is not that a leader is better than a manager. Truth – we need both doing what they do best. But not having a clear understanding of their respective roles creates confusion and conflict.

And when they support each other, the organization has an increased opportunity for accelerated growth and sustainable success.

The right stuff

Leaders have most of the following qualities: visionary, passionate, focused, interrelating, communicators (including listening), creative, open, collaborative, decisive, flexible, courageous, power by demonstration. Above all, they are authentic.

Managers have many of these characteristics: logical, persistent, interactive, problem solving, methodical, organized, assertive, operational, systematic, trusting and trustworthy, power by position. Most of all, they are action oriented.

Leaders do the right thing. Managers do things right. – Peter Drucker, management consultant, educator, author.

Out of management, into leadership

What to do if you are too busy managing so that you cannot be leading? These are some ideas:

- Delegate managerial tasks to managers and follow up on their commitments.
- Examine your daily "to do" list and ask if you are managing or leading.
- Ask those you are leading what they think about your leadership.
- Get more training about how to be a good leader.
- Use a formal assessment tool to find out more about the quality of your leadership.

And, find a mentor who can steer you into being a better leader. Particularly a mentor who has proven experience in being an effective leader themselves.

The Bottom Lines

Are you leading? Your company, organization, or project? Or, are you drowning in managing and unable to lead? Learn and adopt the characteristics of a good leader. Be the leader you are meant to be. Lead your managers – they are invaluable. Like you.

Index – Topic, Lesson Number

Accountable, 42
Action, 43
Adapter, 41
Adopter, 41
Assumptions, 26
Behaviors, 40
Bigness, 6
Branding, 7
Ceiling, 29
Competition 31
Complaints, 49
Confusion, 50
Connecting, 33, 39
Consciousness, 32
Continuity, 5
Courage, 9, 15, 38
Creative, 37
Critic, 20
Daily, 18
Defy, 27
Demands, 35
Disagreement, 37
Disengagement, 51
Disrespect, 36
Disruption, 32
Drama, 48

Effective, 52
Employees, 1, 51
Encounters, 10
Energy, 4
Essentials, 16
Expectations, 14
Failure, 34, 36
Fast, 30
Fear, 15
Future, 23, 24
Gift, 21
Goals, 14, 25
Gratitude, 18
Gutless, 9
Hammers, 29
Hope, 12
Inner, 20
Insight, 19
Intentions, 35
Kill, 26
Laws, 6
Learn, 19
Loss, 44
Manager, 52
Marketing, 7
Mastery, 5

Maturity, 48
Mediocrity, 42
Mind, 8
Model, 17
Motivation, 11
Myths, 13
Negative, 49
Networking, 33
Neuro-Leadership, 24
New, 8
Offices, 3
Order, 3
Pivot, 17
Problems, 2
Profit, 44, 45
Progress, 30
Purge, 45
Questions, 50
Reality, 12, 13
Receptivity, 21
Reinvention, 22
Repair, 47
Respect, 36
Resume, 23
Simplicity, 16
Skills, 40

Smart, 25
Solutions, 2
Stagnation, 22
Stalling, 43
Success, 1, 4, 38, 46

Synchronicity, 10
Teach, 11
Tyranny, 28
Unawareness, 34
Uncertainty, 27

Uniqueness, 31
Vagueness, 28
Vision, 39, 47

How to Order More Books

The author, Tom Zender, hopes that you enjoyed this book.

Additional copies of both books in this series by Tom Zender are available:
The Bottom Lines 2016: 52 Unforgettable Lessons in Leadership
The Bottom Lines 2017: 52 More Motivating Lessons in Leadership
The Bottom Lines 2018: 52 More Memorable Lessons in Leadership

They can be ordered at www.amazon.com in both the print and digital e-book versions.

Contact the Author
Tom Zender
tomzender@me.com
www.tomzendermentor.com

www.ingramcontent.com/pod-product-compliance
Lightning Source LLC
Chambersburg PA
CBHW052254220526
45471CB00001B/338